A JOURNEY OF RICHES

TAPPING INTO COURAGE

Ten Resourceful Insights

Developing Character to Live Life

A Journey Of Riches - Tapping into Courage
Ten Resourceful Insights
Developing Character to Live Life. © 2018

Published by Motion Media International
Editing: Gwendolyn Parker, Chris Drabenstott.
Cover Design: Motion Media International
Typesetting & Assembly: Motion Media International
Printing: Amazon and IngramSparks

Creator: John Spender - Primary Author
Title: *A Journey Of Riches - Tapping into Courage*
ISBN Digital: 978-1-64516-906-2
ISBN Print: 978-1-64516-905-5
Subjects: Self-Help, Motivation/Inspiration and Spirituality.

ACKNOWLEDGMENTS

Reading and writing is a gift that too few give to themselves. It is such a powerful way to reflect and gain closure from the past, reading and writing is a therapeutic process. The experience raises one's self-esteem, confidence, and awareness of self.

I learned this when I created the first book in the *A Journey Of Riches* series, which is, now one of sixteen books with over 170 different co-authors from thirty-five different countries. It's not easy to write about your own personal experiences and I honor and respect every one of the authors who has collaborated in the series thus far.

For many of the authors, English is their second language, which is a significant achievement in itself. In curating this anthology of short stories, I have been touched by the amount of generosity, gratitude, and shared energy that this experience has given everyone.

The inspiration for *A Journey Of Riches, Tapping into Courage* came from my own experience of tapping into courage. Of course, I could not have created this book without the nine other co-authors who each said YES when I asked them to share their insights and wisdom into their journey of tapping into courage. Just like each chapter in this book makes for inspiring reading, each story represents one chapter in the presence of each of the authors, with the chief aim of having you, the reader, living a more abundant life.

I'd like to thank all the authors for entrusting me with their unique memories, encounters, and wisdom. Thank you for sharing and opening the door to your soul so that others may learn from your experience, may the readers glean confidence from your successes and wisdom from your failures.

Thank you to my family, I know you are proud of me and how far I have come from that 10-year-old boy who was learning how to read and write at a fundamental level. Mom, Robert, Dad, Merril, my brother Adam and his daughter Krystal, my sister Hollie, her partner Brian, my nephew Charlie and my niece, Heidi. Also my grandparents Gran and Pop who are alive and well and Ma and Pa who now rest in peace. They accept me just the way I am with all my travels and adventures around the world.

Thanks to all the team at MotionMediaInternational who have done an excellent job at editing and collating this book. It has been a pleasure working with you all on this successful project, and I thank you for your patience in dealing with the various changes and adjustments along the way.

Thank you, the reader for having the courage to look at your life and how you can improve your future in a fast and rapidly changing world.

And I'd enjoy connecting with readers, as I love sharing stories.

You can email me here: jrspender7@gmail.com

Thank you again to my fellow co-authors: Francisca X Ruiz, Neelu Parihar, Hamichand Haimer Katwaroo, Theresa Rodriguez, Frances Loughrey, Donna Pearl, Susan Campbell Nickels, Alice Ho and Laura Hyman.

I hope you have enjoyed this co-authored experience as much as I have.

With gratitude,
John Spender

PRAISE FOR *A JOURNEY OF RICHES* BOOK SERIES.

"The *A Journey Of Riches* book series is a great collection of inspiring short stories that will leave you wanting more!"
~ Alex Hoffmann, Network Marketing Guru.

"If you are looking for an inspiring read to get you through any change, this is it!! This book is filled with many gripping perspectives, from a collection of successful international authors with a tonne of wisdom to share."
~ Theera Phetmalaigul, Entrepreneur/Investor.

"*A Journey Of Riches* is an empowering series that implements two simple words in overcoming life's struggles.

By diving into the meaning of the words "problem" and "challenge," you will find yourself motivated to believe in the triumph of perseverance. With many different authors from all around the world, coming together to share different stories of life's trials, you will find yourself drenched in encouragement to push through even the darkest of battles.

The stories are heartfelt personal shares of moving through and transforming challenges into rich life experiences.

The book will move, touch and inspire your spirit to face and overcome any of life's adversities. A truly inspirational read. Thank you for being the kind open soul you are John!!"
~ Casey Plouffe, Seven Figure Network Marketer.

"A must-read for anyone facing major changes or challenges in life right now. This book will give you the courage to move through any challenge with confidence, grace, and ease."
~ Jo-Anne Irwin - Transformational Coach & Best Selling Author.

"I'm a fan of self-help books, and I read them a lot. I love this book and the stories that are contained within them, but most of all I like the concept. I love that John Spender decided to do an anthology of stories from inspirational people. This book is the type of book where you can either choose to be inspired by ten different stories or choose a chapter that resonates with you the most.

As I read this book, it confirmed to me my life suspicion that things happen beyond our control. It can be incredibly devastating at times. It is those moments that bring us to our knees not knowing whether we can or even want to stand anymore. But, in these challenging moments, this book confirms to me that we do have one choice we can let go, make changes and embrace the new. It's the choice of how we decide to view these hardships. Our perspective determines what our life will be after these moments in our lives.

Some very heart-wrenching stories were contained in these books. Some of them I even had to ask myself, "How do you even recover from a situation like that?"

Perspective. It all boils down to how we decide to view those hard challenges that come our way. At least that is what I took away from this book.

Thank you to John and his team of authors for getting together to create this book."
~ Kit Zakimi on Amazon.

"I have enjoyed the *Journey of Riches* book series. Each person's story is written from the heart and everyone's journey different. We all have a story to tell, and John Spender does an amazing job of finding authors and combining their stories, into uplifting books."
~ Liz Misner Palmer, Foreign Service Officer.

"A timely read as I'm facing a few changes right now. I liked the various insights from the different authors. This book will inspire you to move through any challenge or change that you are experiencing."
~ David Ostrand, Business Owner.

"I've known John Spender for a while now, and I was blessed with an opportunity to be in book four in the series. I know that you will enjoy this new journey like the rest of the books in the series. The collection of stories will assist you with making changes, to deal with challenges and to see that transformation is possible for your life."
~ Charlie O'shea, Entrepreneur.

"A Journey of Riches series will draw you in and help you dig deep into your soul. Every author has an unbelievable life story of purpose inside of them. John Spender is dedicated to bringing peace, love, and adventure to the world of his readers! Dive into this series, and you will be transformed!!"
~ Jeana Matichak, Author of Finding Peace.

"Awesome! Truly inspirational! It is amazing what the human spirit can achieve and overcome! Highly recommended!!"
~ Fabrice Beliard, Australian Business Coach, and Best Selling Author.

"*A Journey of Riches* Series is a must read. It is an empowering collection of inspirational and moving stories full of courage, strength, and heart. Bringing peace and awareness to those lucky enough to read to assist and inspire them on their life journey."
~ Gemma Castiglia, Avalon Healing, Best Selling Author.

"The *A Journey of Riches* book series is an inspirational collection of books that will empower you to take on any challenge or change in life."
~ Kay Newton, Midlife Stress Buster, and Best Selling Author.

"*A Journey of Riches* book series is an inspiring collection of stories, sharing many different ideas and perspectives on how to overcome challenges, deal with change and to make empowering choices in your life. Open the book anywhere and let your mood chose where you need to read. Buy one of the books today; you'll be glad that you did! "
~ Trish Rock, Modern Day Intuitive, Bestselling Author, Speaker, Psychic & Holistic Coach.

"Transformational Change is another inspiring read in the *A Journey of Riches* book series. The authors are from all over the world, and each has a unique perspective to share, that will have you thinking differently about your current circumstances in life. An inspiring read!"

~ Alexandria Calamel, Success Coach and Best Selling Author.

"The A Journey of Riches books is a collection of real-life stories, which are truly inspiring and give you the confidence that no matter what you are dealing with in your life, that there is a light at the end of the tunnel, and a very bright one at that. Totally empowering!"
~ John Abbott, Freedom Entrepreneur.

"An amazing collection of true stories from individuals who have overcome great changes and who have transformed their lives and used their experience to uplift, inspire and support others."
~ Carol Williams, Author-Speaker-Coach.

"You can empower yourself from the power within this book, that can help awaken the sleeping giant within you. John has a purpose in life to bring inspiring people together to share their wisdom, for the benefit of all who venture deep into this book Transformational Change. If you are looking for inspiration to be someone special in this book can be your guide."
~ Bill Bilwani, Renown Melbourne Restaurateur.

"In the A Journey Of Riches series, you will catch the impulse to step up, reconsider and settle for only the very best for yourself and those around you. Penned from the heart and with an unflinching drive to make a difference for the good of all, *A Journey Of Riches* series is a must-read."
~ Steve Coleman Author of "Decisions, Decisions! How to Make the Right One Every Time."

"If you want to be on top of your game? *A Journey of Riches* is a must read with breakthrough insights that will help you do just that!"
~ Christopher Chen, Entrepreneur.

"In *A Journey of Riches*, you will find the insight, resources, and tools you need to transform your life. By reading the authors stories, you too can be inspired to achieve your greatest accomplishments and what is truly possible for

you. Reading this book activates your true potential for transforming, you're life way beyond what you think is possible. Read it and learn how you too can have a magical life."
~ Elaine Mc Guinness, Bestselling Author of Unleash Your Authentic Self!

"If you are looking for an inspiring read look no further than the *A Journey Of Riches* book series. The books are an inspiring collection of short stories, that will encourage you to embrace life even more. I highly recommend you read one of the books today!"
~ Kara Dono, Doula, Healer and Best Selling Author.

"*A Journey of Riches* series is a must-read for anyone seeking to enrich their own lives and gain wisdom through the wonderful stories of personal empowerment & triumphs over life's challenges. I've given several copies to my family, friends, and clients to inspire and support them to step into their greatness. I highly recommend that you read these books, savoring the many aha's and tools you will discover inside."
~ Michele Cempaka, Hypnotherapist, Shaman, Transformational Coach & Reiki Master.

"If you are looking for an inspirational read, look no further than the *A Journey Of Riches* book series. The books are an inspiring and educational collection of short stories from the author's soul itself, that will encourage you to embrace life even more. I've even given them to my clients too so that they are inspired by their journeys in life, wealth, health and everything else in between.

I recommend you make it a priority, to read one of the books today!"

~ Goro Gupta, Chief Education Officer, Mortgage Terminator, Property Mentor.

"The *A Journey Of Riches* book series is filled with real-life short stories of heartfelt tribulations turned into uplifting, self-transformation by the power of the human spirit to overcome adversity. The journeys captured in these books will encourage you to embrace life in a whole new way.

I highly recommend reading this inspiring anthology series."
~ Chris Drabenstott, Best Selling Author, and Editor.

"There is so much motivational power in the *A Journey of Riches* series!! Each book is a compilation of inspiring, real-life stories by several different authors, which makes the journey feel more relatable and success more attainable. If you are looking for something to move you forward, you'll find it in one (or all) of these books."
~ Cary MacArthur, Personal Empowerment Coach

"I've been fortunate to write with John Spender and now call him a friend. *A Journey of Riches* book series features real stories that have inspired me and will inspire you. John has a passion for finding amazing people from all over the world, giving the series a global perspective on relevant subject matters."
~ Mike Campbell, Fat Guy Diary, LLC

"The *A Journey of Riches* series, is the reflection of beautiful souls who have discovered the fire within. Each story takes you inside the truth of what truly matters in life. While

reading these stories, my heart space expanded to understand that our most significant contribution in this lifetime is to give and receive love. May you also feel inspired as you read this book."
~ Katie Neubaum, Author of Transformation Calling.

"A Journey of Riches is an inspiring testament that love and gratitude are the secret ingredients to living a happy and fulfilling life. This series is sure to inspire and bless your life in a big way. Truly an inspirational read, written and created by real people, sharing real-life stories about the power and courage of the human spirit."
~ Jen Valadez, Emotional Intuitive, and Best Selling Author

TABLE OF CONTENTS

Acknowledgments.. iii

Praise for *A Journey Of Riches* book series...................................v

Preface.. 1

Chapter One: Courage Is A Muscle

    By John Spender 5

Chapter Two: Courage Doesn't Always Roar

    By Frances Loughrey 17

Chapter Three: Surrendering to Courage

    By Francisca X Ruiz 31

Chapter Four: Courage

    By Laura Hyman..45

Chapter Five: The Life of Dr. Neelu A Story of Courage

    By Neelu Parihar 57

Chapter Six: Rays Of Courage

    By Susan Campbell Nickels 69

Chapter Seven: Sink or Swim

    By Haimchand Katwaroo................................83

Chapter Eight: Finding The Courage To Be My Authentic Self

By Theresa Rodriguez *101*

Chapter Nine: The Courage to Move

By Donna Pearl *113*

Chapter Ten : Courage In Everyday Life

By Alice Ho *125*

Author Biographies

John Spender 137

Frances Loughrey 139

Francisca X Ruiz 141

Laura Hyman 143

Dr. Neelu Parihar 144

Susan Campbell Nickels 145

Haimchand Katwaroo 147

Theresa Rodriguez 149

Donna Pearl 150

Alice Ho 151

Afterword 153

PREFACE

I created this book and chose this collection of authors to share their insights, into their journey of developing courage, assisting people and raising your belief that you too can tap into courage and overcome your fears.

Like all of us, each author has a unique story and insight to share with you. It just may be the case, that one or more of these authors have lived through an experience that is similar to circumstances in your life right now. Their words could be just the words you need to read to help you through your challenges and motivate you to continue on your journey. Perhaps reading about one or more of these experiences will fill in the missing piece of your puzzle, so to speak, allowing you to move forward into the next phase of your life.

Storytelling has been the way humankind has communicated ideas and learning throughout our civilization. While we have become more sophisticated with technology and living in the modern world is more convenient, there is still much discontent and dissatisfaction with one's reality. Many people have also moved away from reading books, and they are missing out on valuable information that can help them to move forward in life, with a positive outlook. I think it is essential to turn off the T.V., to slow down, and to read, reflect, and take the time to appreciate everything you have in life.

I like anthology books because they carry many different

perspectives and insights on a singular topic. I find that sometimes when I'm reading a book that has just one author I gain an understanding of their viewpoint and writing style very quickly and the reading becomes predictable. With this book and all of the books in the *A Journey of Riches* book series, you have many different writing styles and viewpoints that will help shape your perspective towards your current set of circumstances.

Anthology books are also great because you can start from any chapter and gain a valuable insight or a nugget of wisdom without the feeling that you have missed something from the earlier chapters.

I love reading many different types of personal development books because learning and personal growth are vital to me. If you are not learning and growing, well, you're staying the same. Everything in the universe is growing, expanding, and changing. If we are not open to different ideas and different ways of thinking and being, then we can become close-minded.

The concept of this book series is to open you up to different ways of perceiving your reality, to give you hope, to encourage you, and to give you many avenues of thinking about the same subject. My wish for you is to feel empowered to make a decision that will best suit you in moving forward with your life. As Albert Einstein said, **"We cannot solve problems with the same level of thinking that created them."**

With Einstein's words in mind, let your mood pick a chapter in the book or read from the beginning to the end and allow yourself to be guided to find the answers you seek.

With gratitude,
John Spender

CHAPTER ONE

COURAGE IS A MUSCLE

By John Spender

I was sitting on the toilet seat with the lid down, still wearing my board shorts and staring at the grey contemporary tiles in my outdoor bathroom in Sanur, Bali. The neighbor's 10 or so birds were chirping away while hanging in their Mango tree. I was preparing myself to record my first ever breathing meditation. My feet were flat on the floor, the larger tiles mixed with volcanic stones in-between, keeping mindful not to drop my mobile phone with my shaking hand. I hit the record button.

We were getting ready to launch Book Three in the *A Journey of Riches* series, "Making Changes," in which I was collaborating with 12 other authors from six different countries. Part of the book launch was to have each co-author to give a gift, so when readers downloaded the book, they would receive a ton of value and not just a book. We made it even more challenging by not allowing anyone to give away a free coaching session, as half of the authors in the book were coaches. As part of the launch, readers were also getting a copy of the first two books as well. It was a challenge to think of what I could gift for the value add.

When you are productive, I think it is advantageous to break up your production cycles with some form of activity to maintain a healthy state of mind throughout the day. I have been meditating for many years now, and I've developed my own breathing technique that takes about 11 minutes and creates a blissful state of clarity. I had only really used it for myself and had never thought about sharing it with the world. Once I came to grips and got over myself with the understanding that this gift could make a difference in someone else's life, I was able to record the meditation while keeping my ever-present nerves under control.

I played back the recording as I chuckled with surprise at how good it sounded, especially with the neighbor's birds naturally chirping in the background. A few months later, after a successful book launch receiving #1 honors in a bunch of countries, one of my co-authors, Casey Plouffe, contacted me after using the meditation and requested that I teach it at her retreat in the States later in the year.

"When you go out of your comfort zone and it works there's nothing more satisfying."

~ Kristen Wiig

More often than not, we are rewarded when we summon the courage to leave our comfort zones for the greater good of humanity. This is one of the best forms of win/win scenarios you can experience. Fear and trepidation are replaced with confidence and a justified sense of elevation. There is so much personal growth to experience when we choose the courageous path, taking a chance on ourselves, daring to risk it all, dying to the illusion of safety.

In his book, *Secrets of the Millionaire Mind*, T Harv Ecker recommends patting yourself on the back and telling yourself, "It's okay; you're growing" any time you get outside your comfort zone and move towards your dream. Having done almost all of Harv's trainings, I've personally heard him share that when he sets goals, no matter how small, he pats himself on the back and says, "Well done, Harv! You did well." This anchors the goal into his subconscious mind. I learned this principle from my days of teaching Christopher Howard's NLP trainings in Singapore. Self-praise is necessary for increased personal growth, and that's why positive self-talk is valuable and a rare character trait. Celebrating your wins, no matter how small, is one of the fastest ways to fast-track and maintain high levels of self-esteem.

Say Yes to Opportunities That Scare You

Here I was in the States with Casey. We had just experienced Sedona with another friend, having the best time trekking through the park. I was feeling a little nervous about teaching the breathing technique that I had basically made up. Casey had told another friend how amazing my breathing meditation was, and he wanted me to lead a session with the speakers of his retreat as well. Naturally, I said yes, trusting that everything would work out.

I had time to sit with the idea as we hiked around the incredible red rock formations with a guide, who also showed us ancient Native American rock paintings. It was here that Casey suggested that I do a breathing session. Agreeing, I didn't tell her that this would be my very first time doing it with a group, even though there was just the four of us. Of course, I was nervous but considered it good practice before the first retreat in a few days in St George, Utah.

During the breathing session at the ancient site, a gust of wind came from nowhere and suddenly stopped. It felt like the magical presence of spirit reminding us that we were on sacred grounds. It became a topic of conversation afterward, as each of us was feeling grateful, realizing what a privilege it was to be hiking in this protected area closed to the general public.

Personally, I feel there is a common global misconception in society about what it means to be courageous, at least in the countries where I travel on trips around the world. It may be different in various indigenous cultures. Most people think that you have to do a heroic act to be considered courageous. In my world, anyone who steps outside his comfort zone in pursuit of his or her passion is an everyday hero, making that person brave. Cemeteries around the world are filled with people who didn't live their love, choosing not to go for their dreams, not taking a chance on themselves to create a better reality for all that walk this earth. Courage is the ability to get outside your comfort zone and do the things that bring you joy.

"It takes courage to grow up and become who you really are."

~ E. E. Cummings

The drive to Utah was a long one. We felt grateful to have arrived safely, narrowly missing a deer that sprinted across the road. After a day of filming, we went hiking with a healer friend of Casey's into one of the many nature reserves in St George. After a few hours of walking into a pretty canyon, Casey suggested I take everyone through my breathing meditation. Another opportunity to practice before the event, and again the feedback was very positive.

Be Resourceful

Sir Richard Branson is famous for his saying **"If Someone offers you an amazing opportunity and you're not sure**

you can do it say yes - then learn how to do it later!" After reading many of Branson's books, I have discovered that one of his main strengths is his resourcefulness to deliver favorable outcomes out of nowhere. For example, the time he and his wife, Joan, were at some airport in the Caribbean and their flight was canceled, thinking outside the box, Branson inquired about chartering a plane. The cost was something like $30,000, and he drew up a sign stating, "Charter flight to the US—tickets $10,000 each," and he sold about eight seats, pocketing something in the vicinity of $50,000 for his troubles.

I read another story in his book *Losing My Virginity*. Richard and Virgin Records were putting on a sold-out concert for Mike Oldfield's *Tubular Bells*. The problem was, Mike is known as an introvert and suddenly got cold feet and pulled out at the last minute. This would be a disaster for Richard, costing Virgin Records hundreds of thousands of dollars in refunds, not to mention the bad publicity.

Branson knew that he needed to treat the situation delicately or Oldfield would go into hiding. Over the phone, he agreed with Mike's decision to withdraw from the sold-out concert, and he invited Mike over for a drive in his red sports car, a '78 MG convertible or something stylish and flashy like that. Branson suggested that Mike drive, and they went through the countryside talking about anything other than the concert.

On their return to Richard's house, he suggested to Mike that if he did the concert that night, he could keep Branson's sports car. Mike thought about it for a moment and agreed. The next day the London papers reported that it was a performance of a lifetime and the concert received rave reviews. It was Branson's resourcefulness that saved the day.

Where in your life are you faced with a seemingly insurmountable challenge? And how can you play it to your advantage, impacting the greater good of all?

I arrived at the Follow Your Bliss retreat early to take the leadership team through my mini breathwork session. Comprising of about 12 people, we went on an 11-minute journey together. The positive feedback I received from everybody was just the boost that I needed. I was also invited to speak the next day about my experience casting a vision for the film I have written and produced. To my surprise, the audience was transfixed on my every word and, feeling inspired, a few audience members bought the A Journey of Riches books and asked for my **autograph**. It was a surreal experience birthed from a breathing meditation I did in my outdoor bathroom while sitting on the toilet. The synchronicities that followed were incredible and beyond my wild imagination; I couldn't have planned the wonder even if I'd wanted to. As they say in the spirituality movement, let go and let God.

"Courage is not the absence of fear, but rather the judgment that something else is more important than fear."

~ Ambrose Redmoon

Spending a relaxing few days with Casey and her husband, Mike, at their lakeside home in Fayetteville, North Carolina, was the perfect way to process the previous week and mentally prepare for her five-day You Can Have It All retreat in Hilton Head, South Carolina. This retreat was, as expected, another fantastic experience of being surrounded by positive people who all wanted to improve their lives on some level. I was running a breathwork session every morning while the sun came up over the ocean, plus sessions in the evenings as well. The breathing sessions were a highlight of the retreat for many of the 50-odd people in attendance. I kept getting asked for a recording, and so, by request, I made a YouTube video of my breathing meditation for everyone that attended the retreat. You can watch it here https://www.youtube.com/watch?v=WONeBxakezl&t=180s. I hope you allow this free recording to take you to a state of bliss. If you can get into the habit of listening to it every morning before you begin the day, delight as you watch the synchronicities flow into your life.

Meeting the skilled and talented trainer, Rod Hairston, was another highlight of the retreat. Rod led the retreat on the last two days. We got on well, although I was in awe whenever I was in his presence. He sat down next to me at a restaurant in town on the last night of the retreat and asked what I did and suggested we collaborate together sometime. I told him about the film, who was in it, and the next minute I was organizing a trip and film shoot in his home just outside Austin, Texas.

Filming Rod was both a challenging and insightful experience. It was challenging in that Rod had assured me that he had a mini studio in his home where they recorded all the company online training videos, but it turned out that their camera wasn't a 4k video recorder, so at the last minute I had to look for someone else. We only had a small window for recording, because Rod had to facilitate training in Michigan and I had a return flight to Bali, Indonesia. I had a green screen that I traveled with, and Rod's team had excellent lighting and a boom mic. We just needed a high-quality camera.

I had heard about thumbtack.com from a previous trip to the States. The predicament being the scheduled shoot was the next day, I received two quotes to do the filming. The work of one of the videographers looked really good. He responded to my messages quickly and the shoot was booked.

When he rocked up the day of the shoot, he didn't have the camera we had agreed upon. He stank of cigarettes and alcohol, but at least he was on time. It turned out the camera he had was much better, but I wasn't sure if the color would match the rest of the footage we already had. When you chose courage over fear, it doesn't mean you won't still have challenges, but generally you will be in a more empowered mindset to deal with them as they arise.

"Courage is the commitment to begin without any guarantee of success."

~ Johann Wolfgang Von Goethe

Having a front-row seat and asking Rod questions as he stared down the barrel of the lens was a magical experience, and time sped by. In no time at all the shoot was done. The videographer had assured me and promised that the footage would be outstanding, and he would color-code it to the existing footage that I had. He was also willing to wait for payment so I could check with my editor as well. During the setup, I knew he was good just by the way he thought while navigating the space we had for the shoot.

Everything worked out in the end, and to believe that this shoot came about from me deciding to record and share a breathing meditation in my outdoor bathroom, opening the door to a series of synchronicities! Naturally, my month in the States wasn't without challenges, but they were fun challenges to overcome. It requires some resourcefulness and a good support network, and you don't always feel ready; but when you take that leap of faith, more often than not, your wings appear. Of course, it also helps when the people around you want to see you succeed.

My team and I are currently preparing to shoot the reenactments for the film this June 2019 in Los Angeles with a top up-and-coming director, James Cullen Bressack. The film is called *Adversity,* and James comes from a family that has made its mark in the movie industry. His dad, Gordon, is an Emmy Award-winning writer, and his mom, Ellen, is a voice actress.

Although he only lasted one month in film school, James has gone on to direct or produce more than 15 Hollywood films, including *Hate Crime, Gangster Land, From Jennifer,* and many more. He shot his first movie on an iPhone with a budget of only seven thousand dollars. Not long after he walked out of film school, he received a call from the cafe where he worked part-time and was asked to go in to work. When Bressack explained to the owner that he was making a movie, the owner told him that he needed to decide whether he was going to make low-budget films or earn real money. James used that conversation as motivation, and he went as far as getting a tattoo of life across his knuckles. The logic is that he wouldn't be able to get a regular job with a tattoo on his hand, and every time he looks down, he's reminded of what he came here to do. Today, at age 26, Bressack is one of the youngest prolific filmmakers in Hollywood.

Most of my friends who are living on purpose deliberately put themselves in situations where safety scares them. What do I mean? Well, if someone is a successful yoga teacher and wants to start running lifestyle retreats, the mindset of my friends would be to start researching and taking public speaking classes so to strengthen up their presenting skills when they're not on a yoga mat. Courage is a muscle, and it is developed through use. All too often, I feel that people fear Fear.

Will Smith has said that he is motivated by fear. The reporter asked him, "What do you mean?" And I remember him saying something like, "I'm terrified by fear; anything that scares me, I do it until the fear is gone." That is a great attitude to have, and no wonder he is such a huge success today. Will recently bungee jumped out of a helicopter for his 50th birthday. Talk about facing your fears!

I'm not talking about adrenaline sports here; I'm talking about everyday activities, the actions you should be doing on a daily basis but don't—the actions that will build your business or find your ideal partner. You really need to value the benefit of getting outside your comfort zone. One of the keys to developing courage is doing things that safely scare you. Another way you expand your courage muscle is to create habits that build solid foundations for your life. Being able to manage your emotions is helpful when taking healthy risks in your life. You start by making the foundation the moment you wake up. If you can win the first hour of your day, then it's easier to win the rest of your day.

"Be brave. Even if you're not, pretend to be. No one can tell the difference."

~ **H** Jackson Brown Jr

In many of her interviews, the late author, poet, and civil rights activist Maya Angelou used to say that when she is facing the world she is not standing alone. Maya used to imagine that all of her ancestors were standing behind her, supporting her in the many endeavors that she was involved in.

All too often, we play the game of life way too safe, in the process undervaluing the difference we make in the lives of others. There is something more important than fear, and when you focus on what matters, you never know where life will take you. I would never have thought that recording my breathing meditation in my outdoor bathroom on the toilet seat would result in an epic adventure around the States. Take a chance on yourself. Cemeteries around the world are filled with people who didn't take a chance on themselves.

Go slowly if you must. Step-by-step progress is better than no progress at all. Most importantly, you will be developing your courage muscle by taking healthy risks and living into the expanded intelligence of life, trusting your intuition. And it all starts with courage.

"Be Brave,
my heart.
Have courage,
My soul."

~ Unknown

CHAPTER TWO

COURAGE DOESN'T ALWAYS ROAR

By Frances Loughrey

In my family, a big Christmas TV favourite was the 1939 film adaptation of *The Wizard of Oz* starring Judy Garland in the lead role of Dorothy. I loved the Cowardly Lion. I thought he was funny. When Dorothy and her companions, Scarecrow and Tinman, encounter him in the forest, he acts all tough, daring them to "put 'em up" and fight with a sort of American gangster accent. They are already scared because they have imagined all sorts of terrifying possibilities for danger in the forest, lions being only one of them. However, the scary lion isn't very scary at all, and when Dorothy stands up to him and calls him out as a coward, we discover that he "even scares himself." He feels ashamed of this because he is meant to be King of the Forest and should not be afraid of anything or anyone. So he accompanies Dorothy, Scarecrow, and Tinman to the Emerald City to ask the Wizard to grant him courage.

When I found myself, at the age of 24, on my own with all the pressure of bringing up three young children, I was terrified. I was terrified of getting it wrong, of not being able to manage, of missing out on life, of failing. I needed some courage. But where would I get it from? I had to learn pretty quickly how to survive. My youngest was only months old and I couldn't go to work yet. I had to put on a good face, though. How would it help my children or me for my fears to monopolise our lives?

This was the beginning of one of my greatest triumphs as a scaredy cat pretending to be King – or Queen – of the Forest. Learning to be tough seemed imperative. I had entered a world that my upbringing hadn't equipped me for. As the children were too young for school, I had no alternative but to seek help from the state. It was a rude awakening and one where I learned to deal with the humiliation and judgement of what it felt like to be categorised as a single-mother scrounger and on the fringes of what society deemed successful. This is not a rags-to-riches story or a near-death experience. It's a regular common garden-variety story, and I'm sure you'll recognise parts of it in your own account or in the stories of people you know. It is the tale of how a scaredy cat found her courage.

I knew I did not want to live on handouts for the rest of my life, nor did I want this to be the example I offered my children. But they were still very young, and childcare would have cost me more than I could have earned. I had to wait. I didn't like to wait. I didn't like it one little bit. My self-worth was so wrapped up in what others thought of me as a person, a mother, a contributor to society, that I struggled with feelings of inadequacy and self-loathing. I felt quite overwhelmed with the enormity of what I needed to do. I felt the fear of social castigation as well as the social judgement of my mothering abilities.

To cope, I chose to focus on specific areas that I felt were priorities. I felt a compelling need to put my energies into a brighter future for all of us. That's what I did. I got my degree and I scrabbled my way into a career that had the potential for me to achieve this higher goal for us all. I fought down my fears; just held my nose and jumped most of the time. I kept the mask of capability and invulnerability firmly attached and convinced many people that my confidence was real, while down in my stomach I felt the churn of unheeded needs being pushed down into the darkness.

To continually force fear down, like a giant float in a swimming pool, takes a great deal of energy. It was hard to maintain that level of energy across all aspects of my life, so I looked to shut down some of them. The easy target was the one that held the most fear and that would require a lot of energy: intimate relationships. Although this certainly did not mean that I had no love in my life, or fun, or relationships, it did mean that I always held back a part of myself, never fully committing or trusting. I thought, at the time, this was merely my ability to trust other people, but I came to realise it was really about my ability to trust myself.

When trust goes, it affects our sense of belonging and engagement as well, because trust is so fundamental to having meaningful and caring relationships. Sometimes, it can also change our understanding of our value, too, which I have already indicated was something I was battling with and having to fake a lot of the time. When we ignore our own emotional and psychological needs, there is a price to pay.

I also shut down a lot of empathy. This was directed mostly at myself; I just did not give myself a break. By that, I mean I was intolerant and unforgiving of my perceived failings. I desperately wanted to escape the feeling of being a failure. Here I was, so young and already stuck in a life of responsibility I hadn't planned. I decided that my softer nature was letting us all down and should be driven out as quickly as possible. It was the strong who survived, right? Survival of the fittest, I thought, buying into this misrepresented quote from Darwin. After all, it was the 1980s: Thatcher was in, the once mighty unions would fall, the two-parent family was idealised, greed was good. It was a dog-eat-dog world; I'd better toughen up or be eaten.

Fear can take many forms. Sometimes, it is imagined – the fear of fear itself. Sometimes, it is the real fear for safety or security. Sometimes it's a convincing blend! Having managed to establish forward motion, working in spite of my fear, armoured with my mask of toughness and invulnerability, I was looking fear in the face and winning. I thought.

Four years later, and in my second year at university, I became ill. My body was going into some lockdown; I was pushing it too hard. My joints swelled so much that I couldn't bend them. I had no strength. I couldn't even tie shoelaces or pull on my clothes. Now, I was terrified. I was scared for myself, for what this would mean for my plans, what it would say about me. It became hard to keep up the appearance of being invincible when it was clear that I could not even do the simplest of ordinary tasks.

It was ages before the doctors would diagnose an arthritic condition linked to my psoriasis. I hadn't even heard of the possibility of that. Sickening waves of outrage and fear would sometimes threaten to derail me entirely. Who would take care of my children? I couldn't even take care of myself anymore. What sort of future would we have? I had to reach out for help. This was a bitter pill to swallow – and there were quite a few pills I had to take during this time. Some required water and others required humility and acceptance – not attributes I'd tapped into a lot lately!

I needed to find more courage but just felt so scared about what the future would now hold. That's when one of my favourite quotes became a bit of a mantra for me, even ending up on my bedroom wall as a reminder:

"Courage is not the absence of fear; it is the making of action in spite of fear, the moving out against the resistance engendered by fear in the unknown and into the future."

~ M Scott Peck

It was reassuring to consider that my decisions to push on regardless of my fear were examples of courage. I had been doing that already. Yes, now I needed to dig deeper for some more; perhaps the amount of courage we can exercise is commensurate with the amount of fear we have. Maybe it's there alongside, but we don't allow ourselves time to see it. Instead, we run blindly into worst-case scenarios and anxiety-ridden solution-seeking preoccupation. When what we need—really need—is to slow down enough to be able to see a broader self and gain a helpful perspective.

I hadn't quite learned the lessons of this well enough during my previous experiences, so here came the universe with a refresher course. But it was more than that. It was a reminder that there was more to creating a fulfilling life than just pounding through. The more force used to push on to a future vision, the more the present moment seemed to protest. I was forced to slow down, to accept help, to admit my vulnerability. I wish I could say that this lesson needed only to come around once for me to shed my emotional armour, but that would be untrue. It did, however, help me to realise that I needed to pay more attention to my body, my needs, and what was happening now as well as what might be possible in the future.

Over the years, this physical condition has improved so much that no one would ever guess that, at one stage in my life, I could not walk properly, dress, or feed myself without pain. My fear around my health might have stopped me in my tracks, but it was actually taking action to mitigate the impact that helped me move forward. My progress was slowed, but not halted. I took great care to avoid putting my body under too much pressure. The fear of returning to that incapacitated state remained with me for years, encouraging me to lead a less active life, but it didn't stop me. It was in the moving forward, taking action, and sheer bloody-mindedness that courage was allowed to surface.

Back on the yellow brick road, Dorothy and her motley crew of friends face a slew of danger-ridden challenges. They choose to dig deeper for their courage while facing haunted forests, malicious flying monkeys, and, of course, the wicked witch. Ultimately, when Cowardly Lion has the opportunity to ask the Wizard for courage, he receives a medal he can wear on his chest, but he is also given a lesson about what courage is and is shown that he can—and does—already access it. He hadn't recognised this in himself, and with this realisation comes a different perspective for the audience as well as for him.

We also have a glimpse into a broader idea of courage. As if to emphasise the point further, when Dorothy asks the Wizard if he was scared when his hot air balloon went off course bringing him to the Land of Oz, he replies, "Scared? You are talking to a man who has laughed in the face of death, sneered at doom, chuckled at catastrophe. I was petrified!" We see the man behind the façade of the Great and Powerful Oz, another example of a robust and fearless external image that belies the truth of what we all feel, be it at different times and in different ways—fear.

I have often been called courageous or brave. Sometimes, that feels quite uncomfortable for me to hear. That's because

I see my fears alongside my courage and know how close I've come to allowing those to submerge everything else. Over time, I've come to realise that feeling fear doesn't negate my courage. I've come to appreciate that recognising and accepting my fear helps me to tap into courage more, because I can see the value of my fear more clearly.

Fear was often my motivator. It was my determination to move away from the fear of remaining the same, of not being enough, of having no place or voice in the world that helped build this motivation. But it was courage and purposeful resolve that kept me moving toward something better, even when things became difficult and painful. It was my love for my children and my hope for a more expansive future that helped me bring in courage. Love is also a great motivator. I would venture, the greatest.

It is tempting to see courage and fear as opposites, but this is not the case. What would you need courage for if you felt no fear? You would not be worried about the consequences of your actions or decisions; you would not care what others thought; you would not have concerns about negative repercussions. You would not be scared for your life, your safety, your reputation, your income, your relationships.

Courage is what you need when you strike out and do something you feel is right, best, or good for you in the face of possible pain, disaster, or humiliation. Courage is what you need to step up, step forward, step out.

Looking back, I can see that courage has played an essential role in many of the decisions I have made and had a significant impact on the life I have led. Sometimes courage was required for situations in which I felt I didn't have much control, like when the children were young, or when I became ill. At other times, for situations that I deliberately cultivated or sought out.

After developing a successful career in fundraising, which provided very well for us while the children were growing up, I realised that I was going through the motions, that I didn't have the same drive as before. I didn't want to spend my life doing the same thing just because it had been hard getting there. The children were older now and didn't need me to support them. I had no excuses for not striking out and making a choice that was for me, and only for me. Striving to find a new purpose and meaning for my life became paramount. I concluded that the greatest fears we face are not the fears we can easily see or detect, but the ones masquerading as sensible options.

So, I decided to have my own little trip down the yellow brick lane to Oz. I journeyed to the Land Down Under, to Australia. Perhaps I was looking for a bit of wizardly magic or an adventure that would point the way. Whatever it was, it was my time. I knew it and I could not ignore it. I didn't want to ignore it. Although there was fear involved in leaving my home, family, and friends to move somewhere where I knew no one, interestingly, it's not those fears that I think of when I reflect on moving here.

The recurring theme of many of my fears is that of failure and what the idea of failure meant to me at the time. For a very long time, failure to me meant a great lack, of not getting it right or being right, of not being good enough. Even the dictionary offers definitions that support these ideas: *lack of success, deficiency of desirable quality, not functioning, collapse*. What these definitions can't do, though, is add context.

When a baby starts to turn over, crawl, and eventually walk, it fails over and over before it manages to achieve any of those things successfully. Like courage and fear, there is a relationship between failure and success that is not about one winning out against the other, but of one supporting the other and even helping create the other. It's in the failures that we learn how to be successful – as anyone who has ever achieved any success will tell us.

All of this points to the idea that it is the fear of failure rather than failure itself that is the problem. Millenia of evolution and conditioning means that we are hard-wired to recognise danger and either avoid it or destroy it. Our brains don't understand the difference between real and perceived hazards, and so it wants to protect us from them all. The quickest and most sure-fire way of doing that is for us to feel fear. The physiological responses that come with fear, the fight or flight reaction, is like a smoke alarm that goes off, so we know we have to get out or quell the fire. However, just like the oversensitive smoke alarm that sounds when you fry an egg or blow out a candle, our alarm system can become far too sensitively tuned so that the mere idea or possibility of danger becomes the trigger for escape, attack, or lockdown.

And, where do these ideas originate? In our thoughts. Pure and simple. Imagined scenarios, rehashed and relived experiences, what-if stories: all of these are just in our thoughts, our imagination, our heads. Even the so-called real stories we hear of in the news or from others' experiences still only exist after the event when we give them room in our heads. For this reason, we need to be aware of what we invite into our minds. We need to deliberately choose where we focus our attention and what we spend energy on. The brain needs exercise, but it requires the right kind of exercise to be healthy, just like any other muscle. It also needs nourishment. As adults, we are the ones who provide the nourishment. Every day we can choose to take action that will increase our focus on those things that bring us joy, peace, and fulfilment. Or not.

Yes, yes, I hear you say. What about the times when those thoughts pop into your head and you can't seem to get rid of them? The ones you didn't invite, but they arrived anyway. That's true as well. Thoughts do come. Then they leave. If we let them. When we feed those thoughts, ruminate on what we have made those thoughts mean, we create a sort of petri dish for fear, and then we watch it grow.

Reading something uplifting, turning our thoughts to gratitude, doing meditation or some physical exertion will provide a different environment where fear cannot grow out of control but can become part of a new inner culture. Our thoughts are fleeting things that only exist in our minds. They are not real unless we make them real. We do that by giving them a meaning. When we do that, we create a feeling or emotion around them. That's when we can get into difficulties. Many of the thoughts we already have, those we call painful memories, are such. To be able to recognise ideas for what they are is crucial if we are going to be able to understand where a lot of our fear is created and then come up with a way to manage it which will allow us to incorporate all aspects of who we are.

I have done a lot of work to reclaim those parts of myself I had protected so much earlier in my life. Sometimes this has been painful, but it was necessary in order to develop a genuine and appreciative sense of my worth. I have had to learn to accept all of me. Perhaps that is where the real test of courage lies. To be able to face my pain, my fears, my shame with forgiveness and love is probably the most significant challenge I have had – and, with it, the greatest reward. I like myself so much more. I contribute more. I can be there for others more. I can be more vulnerable, put myself out there, and let go. Just being me feels just fine.

I can understand that to regret the choices I made or the strategies I deployed to survive and to create a more positive future would be not only futile but nonsensical. I did the best I could with what I knew and could deal with at the time. That is all any of us can do. The real courage lies in *not* hiding in safety, reverting to comfort, or colluding with a small vision of ourselves. The steps we take today might seem trivial or even inconsequential, but when we make decisions based on a higher perception of who we are or can be, we steadily become that person.

My future vision is no longer focused on economic stability that means my children can have new toys for Christmas or a career that will provide a future for me, but on how I can tap into what strengths I have and how I can use them in courageous ways to create possibilities and opportunities for others as well as for myself. So, my new quote about courage is from Anais Nin:

"Life shrinks or expands in proportion to one's courage."

Since choosing this new way of being, I have written and published two books, lived a nomadic existence housesitting and/or dog sitting, run workshops for teams in universities and clinical health facilities, been invited to speak to workforces about my work, travelled and stayed in Asia, and currently I am working on getting one of my self-leadership programs online. I have also become more relaxed about screwing up, because I see it in a different light. I don't need to be right all the time, because being right is not part of my worth or identity.

I am not terrified or repulsed by my fears anymore but see them as a natural indicator of something unfamiliar approaching or a healthy warning sign to take a bit of care. I don't feel I have to bury it or defeat it but can acknowledge it and appreciate that it provides me with another opportunity to exercise courage. The more airtime my courage gets, the more I will be able to experience in life. It's what enables me to reach out for the new and exciting and to develop parts of myself that would otherwise slumber.

It seems that life does expand in proportion to one's courage, and one's courage expands when we accept that our fears are merely a part of a process that can create courage if we allow it. I heartily recommend stretching that courage muscle. If you can muster it alongside your fears in full acceptance, you will get the full benefit of the process. However, if your fear still rears too big for you right now to manage that, do what you need to do to flex the muscle.

This is not a perfection-striving action or attitude. Nor is it a one-solution-for-all idea. This is my experience, my story, and my journey. Do not be afraid to create your own. Alternatively, if you are worried, use it as the catalyst to call forth your courage from its hiding place. To end where we came in, with the Cowardly Lion, perhaps he needed to hear this from Mary Anne Radmacher:

"Courage doesn't always roar. Sometimes courage is the little voice at the end of the day that says I'll try again tomorrow."

"It takes courage
to grow up and
become who you
really are."

~ EE. Cummings

CHAPTER THREE

SURRENDERING TO COURAGE

By Francisca X Ruiz

It was a beautiful summer morning, July 6th, 2017. The sun was shining, the birds were singing. Since I was a little girl, I have always loved the summer mornings—the scent in the air, the sun's rays melting the drops off the trees, flowers unto the land and cars in the neighborhood, waking up to the sound of children playing outside. On this particular morning, my heart was rejoicing as my youngest daughter, Ali, was visiting. She had been living for over a year in the jungles of Costa Rica. Having grown up in the concrete jungle, as she called the streets of New York City, she felt like life had no real meaning as she watched the changes of this beautiful, busy city and observed how humanity was increasingly dishonoring this planet called Earth, as well as each other. One day, she said, "Mom, I have to leave. I can't handle staying here any longer."

I am the mother of two amazing women, both having such incredibly different life paths. I was a single mom that was so consumed by life and making sure my daughters where happy. Along the path and the self-inflected stressors, I had lost my soul's purpose. I was a Real Estate Broker in the commercial and investment industry. I would have never allowed myself to share my spirituality because of how I felt my clients would view me. My family was getting my crumbs. I was consumed with how things had to be instead of what my spirit was loudly asking me to be. My oldest daughter, Frankie had moved to Los Angeles. She had the ability to capture people's hearts with her stage presence. Her ability to deliver lines that moved you to the core, and experience her characters' emotions to the deepest level of your soul. She had been the lead in school plays and had continued her education in college as a theater major. Her life took many turns and twists, and her passion for acting was forced to take a back seat when her idol, her love, my mother, was admitted to the hospital. Mom was being treated like a guinea pig. The doctors had no idea what was wrong with her. We just knew she was slowly slipping away from us. At the time, Frankie was attending college in Philadelphia. She couldn't bear to stay away at this junction when her grandma—the woman that made every booboo better and every one of her wishes possible—was facing a most difficult challenge. We didn't know Mom's diagnosis. What could possibly be happening to this amazing woman that had endured so many challenges in her life? Why was God not allowing the doctors and many tests identify her diagnosis? Why did it seem like the world was caving in and there was nothing we could do about it? Within a 90-day period, the life of our idol, our mentor, the woman that had sacrificed her own life to bring us to this country, seemed to be coming to an end.

Mom, or "Chelo," as her friends and family lovingly called her, was misdiagnosed. It was like watching a beautiful rose wilting, being torn from the inside out. Every inch of her started breaking down as we closely watched her for any signs of how we could assist and help her heal. The whole family came together. We prayed for everything that we thought was possible to keep her alive. Why were spirit and the angels that she believed in with every fiber seem so disconnected while she was breaking down?

One cold, October morning, the doctors came in and asked if we should do another bone marrow test. I looked at Mom, and all of a sudden I saw her with her family; I saw her spirit as the beautiful young woman with her long, curly locks playing on her beloved farm in Cuba alongside her siblings. I saw her mother and father looking so healthy and happy, and I knew her time to cross over had arrived. I walked out of the room and ran all over the hospital, eventually ending up outside in the parking lot, gasping for air. My heroine was going to cross over, yet I had so much that I still needed to say and share with her. Who was going to caress my hair when I felt sick? Who was going to cook for the family and give me advice when I felt lost? My mom was always the first person I called in the morning and the last one I called at night, no matter where we were in the world. How was I going to face this next chapter of my life? She was so young, yet her soul had chosen to leave. I came back to the room, and with tears in my eyes, I realized I could not be selfish; she didn't deserve to suffer anymore. She deserved to rest. We held her tightly and watched while the minutes on the clock ticked by and her heart rate reduced to a stop that inevitably led to her last breath.

Love takes us to places and experiences where we want to keep those we love the most near us, but God has a way to send us a message. In Mom's case, a feather is what she chose to give us courage and trust that she was ok. She had been reunited with her family that had crossed over years prior. She deeply missed them, and due to Castro and immigration laws, she was not even able to be present to bury her Mom, Dad, sister and brothers. A couple of days before she crossed over, the family had taken a pillow case and put their fingerprints on it and placed it on her body. It was time for her to rest and not suffer any longer. We were a close-knit Latino family, and we were all devastated, but she had taught us that regardless of the situation, we should always stay together and love each other.

Not long after her beloved Abi passed, my daughter Frankie was getting ready to graduate from college. Frankie was stepping into her most significant role as an actor, and she knew her grandmother would be so proud to watch her embarking into her life's passion. She is raw and intentional, giving the audience an experience where they can feel the story deeply. She has so much to share, as her life has been filled with so many challenges; and her heart is so full of love. Although Mom had moved on, her love and guidance continued to help us on our paths to becoming the women she had envisioned us to be.

My youngest daughter, Ali, was getting ready for her next journey, as she was heading to the Dominican Republic to continue her self-discovery. She had experienced how her soul felt full, waking up in the mornings to the sound of running rivers, oceans, animals singing and running wildly through the jungles of Costa Rica. The feeling of sand on her body after a long day of teaching others how to survive in the jungle, and enjoying farms that became her playground. Her day in the jungle started with a 6 a.m. meditation followed by yoga. I was in awe at how her life had shifted. She was studying to become a yoga instructor and learning about ayurvedic cooking. Her journey in Costa Rica woke up her senses and joy for living a life full of adventure. She came to visit me in NJ. We would practice yoga in the mornings and she would teach me her modalities. Then we'd cook these fantastic recipes with ingredients that made each dish seem like heavenly morsels in your mouth. I could have never imagined Ali cooking up a storm, making these dishes with so much love, using coconut and herbs that made our kitchen smell so amazing. But I knew she was feeling restless in the concrete jungle and was ready for her next journey; it was time to continue on her path.

It was the morning of July 6th when we discussed going for dinner with her friends. I received a call from a friend saying that a poodle was found and they needed someone to watch him until they located his owners. I went to meet the puppy, and a young boy walked in asking to take him. My heart went out to him, as I know how amazing it feels for children to have a pet to love. I had grown up with dogs and my first baby was a grey poodle named Donny after Donny Osmond. He was a fantastic puppy. He knew my deepest secrets and he got me through my darkest moments. The young boy was so happy that he had a new friend there was no way I could keep the puppy the boy deserved the experience of having a puppy.

I started walking back home thinking about the puppy and the joy in the little boy's face. My friend was driving his SUV with his kids and wife and I was goofing around jumping on and off the driver's doors side. We both lived in a gated community where children play outdoors and families know each other. It is a community where we watch over each other's homes and families. He must have been going no more than three to five mph. We were all chatting and laughing and I jumped unto the driver's doors side rail. The kids were laughing so hard watching us being silly and telling stories. He said "you look so happy I'm going to keep driving out of the community." I said "no way I'm heading home, I have to take my daughter and her friends out for dinner." She was traveling to the

Dominican Republic the next day. I thought I was stepping off the driver's door rail. I had always felt I could do stunts that you see in movies. I felt that if in two other occasions I had been able to jump on and off a moving vehicle why not now. His daughter asked her dad where is Franny? He had turned around to speak to his wife when I had stepped off, but this time the universe had another plan. I remember him carrying me home since I was two blocks away from my house when I jumped off and opening my eyes and thinking I was ok. My hands were bleeding, my legs had cuts, my eyebrow had a slash as he carried me into the living room. He asked me if I was ok and all my senses where thinking yes I have to take Ali and her friends out for dinner. The steps into the home seemed like they were moving like an escalator even though they are made of wood. I sat down on the couch and as he called my daughter Ali to come downstairs. I live in a townhome and she was upstairs not knowing that her mom had even left the house to rescue a dog. I'm ok just get me some gauze and peroxide thinking I'll clean my wounds and head out for dinner. Ali comes downstairs and looks at me not understanding what the heck happened. Our sofa faces a red wall where a beautiful painting of the universal mother and fireplace seemed to be moving. As I looked up to pray the room went into a spin that I couldn't stop. I asked my friend and Ali to take me to the emergency room something was happening.

We sat in the ER for over five hours and I felt as if my head was going to explode. It was so busy and noisy until they finally took me in. I was a bit embarrassed as I contemplated how I was going to explain to the doctors what had happened. The doctors took me in to get to CT scan. When they finally returned with the results, they informed me that two areas of my brain were bleeding. I looked at Ali, and all I could think about was how sorry I was that I couldn't keep my word on taking her to dinner. The ER doctor indicated that I would have to be observed for the next 24 hours for signs of dizziness or bleeding. In my heart, I knew I would never allow any procedures. I had witnessed my friend Barbara have her head cut open after an aneurysm and she was never able to take care of herself again. I would prefer to cross over than to be a burden to my children. I had vowed a long time ago that if I couldn't take care of myself, I would prefer to leave this planet.

Ali had her plane ticket for the next day to fly to the Dominican Republic. She was lying on the hospital bed and her eyes were filled with fear and confusion about whether she should stay with me or leave for the Dominican Republic. When she asked me what she should do, my first instinct was to tell her to do what makes her happy. She had a new job there, and I was worried about what her boss would say if she didn't go. As it turned out, she was able to change her flight and wait a few extra days. The hospital released me and indicated that unless I was vomiting or had a fever, the bleeding would stop. We arrived back home and I felt like someone had beaten me up. I went to bed, and when I woke up the following morning, I noticed that I couldn't take a deep breath. I calmly got dressed and asked Ali to call an ambulance—something was not right. I was rushed back to the hospital. The ER nurses asked why I was sent home so quickly. They ran another c-scan and determined that I now had a third area of my brain that was bleeding, apparently caused from sleeping on my back the night before. Once again, they indicated that they would just have to wait and see how I reacted. I didn't have an ounce of energy to request anything from anyone; I knew I needed to shut down. We came back home and this time, I chose to sleep on the couch sitting up since the pressure in my head was eased in a sitting position.

Three days had gone by and it was time for Ali to continue her journey. I knew she needed to go, yet I still wondered how I would be able to take care of myself in this condition. I couldn't walk straight, cook, or do any of the normal things that we often take for granted. I knew she had to leave, but my heart inside desperately wanted her to stay until I was a bit stronger. Ali was resourceful. She started contacting friends and family to line up support for me. She spoke to my cousin Nidia and to my healing support team and they made her feel at ease that I would recuperate fully. Nidia had introduced me to a group of men and women that share a self-development group called Synergy. These magical people had been introduced in my life when I least expected to meet such amazing souls. We all came from such different backgrounds. It was so incredible that such a diverse group of strangers could become closer than any blood family in less than a year's time. They all stepped in when Ali left. Day and night, hey took turns staying with me for two weeks. They fed me and made sure I was comfortable. It was so humbling to have these people who were strangers a year before my accident be the ones that had become my family and saviors.

My body just wanted to rest, but my spirit was traveling to places that I would have never imagined. I was laid out on my couch for over four months. It seemed like the whole world had stopped. What was I supposed to learn from my accident? Why did Spirit, God, Source, the angels stop me in my tracks? I was receiving downloads and traveling out of this realm and didn't know how to explain it or share what I was feeling.

At the time, my dear friend, brother, and mentor, Andreas, was being admitted into the hospital to start his cancer treatments. He is a man that I adored and although I was physically unable to visit him in the hospital, on a spiritual level, I felt so connected to him through his process. I felt as if we were connecting not only when we spoke on the phone for hours, but our souls were traveling through the dimensions, learning and teaching each other lessons that could not have been discovered outside of this experience. We were both going through our individual experiences, yet I felt so connected to his soul. We spoke about what was essential in life and what our purpose was on this planet. You hear people sharing that it takes an experience to stop you in your tracks and boy were my tracks running crazy hours to change.

My cousin Nidia made sure I was recovering well and she would stop by and treat me at home since I couldn't move. I would spend hours visiting with Mom and my ancestors, feeling the joy of being nowhere and everywhere. Having the ability to have conversations with them became the most joyous part of my day. It is amazing the experience of connecting to your family that have crossed over to find the trust and faith that God not only has a perfect plan but when you truly surrender and listen with your heart everything becomes possible.

A few weeks had gone by and I woke up and saw my daughter Frankie's dog, Brando, in the bedroom hallway. Frankie had come to visit as a surprise and brought her dog, who she knew I adored. Like Ali had, Frankie also asked, "Mom, should I stay? You need help." But I was my mom's daughter, and she had taught me to be strong and to trust. We are women that are born to make a difference. I asked Frankie to return to her life and husband and reassured her that I am in God's hands.

I was desperately looking for answers, and one day, I watched this beautiful caterpillar that seemed to be in the same place every morning as I sat on my stoop. (At the time, the stoop was as far as I could walk to outside of the house.) The caterpillar seemed to be moving so gently, yet with such conviction of knowing that it would soon become a beautiful butterfly. It was those moments, my soul would receive more downloads and seeing myself like the butterfly coming out of this state and healed to serve others. I realized my journey as I had known it was changing forever, and I was remembering the lessons my mom had taught me through my years of suffering due to many health challenges and broken hearts. I had been in relationships that I knew had to end yet I fought so hard to make them work. I was on a path where instead of taking time to fall in love with all of me and my soul's journey, I would evaluate my joy because I was loving and loved by another even when that love was not healthy for either one of us. Was the fear of being alone greater than accepting Source's messages to let go and trust? My tribe held space to uncover such deep places that I would not have discovered if it wasn't for my accident and being physically stopped in my tracks.

I left my passion for music to take care of Mom. She had surgery and was not able to take care of herself, which left me having to choose between my music career or taking care of her. Naturally, I chose her. I had married a man because I had gotten pregnant. I knew in our culture I would have caused great pain to my parents reputation in the community so I married him. I was a Cuban woman who was raised old-fashioned, to the point that until I was 18, my brother would have to go with me everywhere, including to my senior prom. I was going to have this child no matter what, so I decided to marry. It was not about the white picket fence and the 2.5 kids that TV portrays; it was about having a loving relationship with a partner you can trust and grow with. This relationship was something that brought the greatest joy to my life with two amazing daughters but I knew it was not able to succeed. If I just stood up and dared to set myself free, things might change. I had accepted his addictions and behavior in hope that he would change. Was I going to repeat history by not listening to spirit, remaining inflexible, arrogant, egoistic, thinking that I was in control? Or had my history and actions given me enough lessons to surrender? I chose to surrender. I chose to listen to the Source, the angels, and Spirit; it was time to begin a new chapter.

This new chapter that I'm now living is humbling. It has offered me a chance to stop and smell the roses, and to trust and listen to the guidance from above. I've been given the courage to feel in all my cells that God has a perfect plan and that everything was working out for me as a complete musical piece. It was my own conversation, for I would never share with my friends or people I would meet that I can channel. I felt that if they knew, they would be judgmental. I was in commercial real estate, which is a male-oriented industry. Even though I came from a lineage of amazing healers and women that channeled Spirit, I didn't want to be put in that box. Since childhood, I was exposed to the many facets of spirituality. I was super afraid of some of them because they included what seemed to me as manipulation. As a teenager, when my connection to Spirit was evolving, I would get totally lost. I would not remember my name or how to return home. All I would remember was to call Mom and she would help. The people my parents knew had various modalities, but they didn't resonate with my soul. I had become paranoid to do anything because of feeling lost. Each experience with spirit because more challenging for I was getting lost not knowing my name or address I just knew to get home to have my families friend help me return to my body and whatever energy was connecting with me released. I had to learn how to maneuver this new situations. It was so overwhelming I became afraid to do things by myself. I began doing prayers and channeling for my family, but after sessions, we all just went on our merry way without any acknowledgment of what had occurred. Mom would just share a bath or anything they might have said to clear my energy. It felt so empty not understanding what was said and how Spirit takes the body and leaves, yet all I know is to take a bath or put flowers to a Saint. Something was missing for me. "Do what you are told and ask no questions" was there motto. My soul had had enough. I did have many questions, and I did want clarity. I could not keep living without understanding how to work with these entities that I was being told was a gift yet they didn't feel like a gift if I was afraid.

I started to meditate and practice yoga, and started seeking through many modalities and religious practices what resonated with my soul. "Will I be ridiculed or accepted?" This was no longer a question; I would just connect and leap into the new space that I had traveled to. I felt like an eagle that had been lovingly watched by its mother and now it was time to throw me out of the nest and allow my wings and spirit to soar. I connected to the beautiful, authentic, loving Source that had brought my soul back to me. The angels, god, Christ energy held me through the darkness and into the light showing me how to allow this beautiful gift to work with me without feeling afraid. Spirit took me from not being able to physically move to not being able to pay my bills into the clarity and the courage that there are no storms without sunshine, followed by a beautiful rainbow where possibility and the many downloads allows for a life that is mindful, and congruent to my beliefs. I'm so grateful for this lesson and so excited for the experience and information downloaded after my brain bled. I'm rejoicing and taking a leap from the highest mountain in trust and gratitude that Source is giving me another chance. I don't have to be ready, I don't have to do anything, I only have to trust, wake up everyday like a child that is excited to play and have the courage that comes with the ability to serve.

There is a saying when life gives you lemons make lemonade. I say when your life goes through challenges that you feel lost and don't know how you are ever going to recover, step into your heart let go and allow source, God, Buddha, Christ energy, Holy Spirit whatever you resonate with. You will feel so much love as they guide and hold you as you gain the courage to live your authentic self. You will be shown your souls purpose and why you are on this beautiful earth will be unveiled giving you permission to continue the journey knowing you are able to go through your darkest moments because you will be risen to your greatest beautiful self.

"Courage is grace
under pressure."

~ Ernest Hemingway

CHAPTER FOUR

COURAGE

By Laura Hyman

It's truly amazing how we are so fearless in the beginning. We learn to walk by falling and getting back up again and again. We learn to talk by saying words over and over till they come out right. We are listening and watching whoever is raising us. We are doing what we see and hear. We don't get to choose a program that we are going to use to create our future selves eventually. We are left learning to hold on to fear. The steps we take in dealing with that fear, however, are our teachers, too.

This is the story of how I learned to let fear run my life until I discovered I had a choice and the ability to change who I want to be. It has taken over fifty years to figure out that I'm in control of what happens in my life.

I was born in 1963, and as a young girl, I grew up in a home where there wasn't much stability. I was faced with a lot of adversities. My parents were both looking to get out of their own negative environments. My father always said that he wasn't good enough to follow in his father's footsteps as a Southern Baptist preacher. He felt he could never make his father happy. My grandmother was the most amazing, kind and strong, loving woman I knew. She worked hard and supported her family, no matter what. My dad felt so unworthy that he started drinking to numb his pain.

My mom was raised by her mother. Her dad disappeared by the time she was two years old. My grandmother packed her up and moved across the country to get away from the very abusive home she had been raised in. She left and never looked back. Then she married two more times and had two sons after my mom. During her second marriage, my mom again found herself in an abusive home. So, until the age of five, I was raised by two adults, both of whom had learned different ways to numb and run from abusive situations in the home.

When I was two and a half, my little brother was born. My mom always said that I was Sam's little protector—his mini mom. She said I did everything for him. He was sick as a baby and ended up having part of one of his lungs removed before he was six months old.

As a five-year-old girl, I remember my parents fighting all the time. Dad had turned to alcohol and drugs by this time and was hardly home, and when he did come home, they fought. I remember a huge fight and my dad trying to stop my mom from yelling at him when he grabbed her and caused her head to hit the refrigerator. That was the last straw for my mom. She packed my brother and me up, and we drove for hours to my grandma's house. When we got there, my grandma was mad and told my mom to go back home and fix her marriage.

When we got back home, Dad was gone. Mom packed us up and we moved back to our hometown. Mom worked two to three jobs at a time. We lived in a tiny town in the Mojave Desert where she worked as a waitress during the day and at the local bar at night. There were times when she had to leave us with whoever she could, and she sometimes made terrible choices when it came to childcare for my brother and me. Sometimes at night she just left us at home sleeping. I remember being scared a lot and unsure who to trust. I cared for my little brother all the time.

Our little town was getting a freeway built right through it. Mom met one of the guys who worked on the freeway project at the bar where she worked at night. She started bringing him around, and he seemed fun and friendly. He was much older than Mom by about 18 years. They went away for a couple of days and came back married. It was great at first to have a dad figure around the house after over three years of not seeing my real dad.

As soon as the freeway was built, we had to move to the next job. Mom's new husband had been married at least four or five times before he married my mom, so we not only got a new dad, but we also got new brothers and sisters. My mom made a point of having his kids come to be with us on holidays and vacations. She blended our family and still worked her butt off waitressing.

My stepdad loved his boats. We spent a lot of time at the river with his friends. It felt perfect to be a part of a family and to get attention from my new dad. That is until he started getting a little too close and began touching me inappropriately and making sure no one else could see. My mom was finally happy with her new family, yet I kept feeling more and more uncomfortable around this man.

We moved a lot; every time a road was done, we had to run again. Because my stepdad worked road construction, when the weather was terrible, he was home. Most of the time, my brother and I were alone with him. Over the years, the touching got worse, and he started to accuse me of sleeping around with boys in our apartment complex. He had convinced me that no one would believe me if I told them what he was doing to me.

He would tell my mom I was doing bad things, which kept me grounded. That's when I started living in fear of being home alone with him. The fear took over my life. I began to find reasons not to be at home. I looked elsewhere for love and a safe place to be. My best friend's house was my safe place. Still, I never told my best friend why I was afraid to go home. I was scared to tell anyone. My mom continued to work all the time; she was hardly ever there.

After a few years, I couldn't take it anymore, so I told her that he was touching me and making me take all my clothes off. She asked me what I wanted her to do. She told me how much she loved him. At the age of eleven, I only wanted my mom to be happy. I was sent to my grandmother's house where no one talked about our problem. It was like nothing had ever happened.

So, I started numbing my pain with alcohol and drugs. And I would do whatever I could not to be home alone with that man. When I came back from my grandmother's, I was subjected to even more fear and abuse. He would search my room and read my diary, and he convinced my mom that I was a whore and a troublemaker.

I stayed grounded all the time. I would leave the house until Mom would get home and then I would be grounded for even longer. As I became older, I would not let my mother's husband come near me. I began to eat and put on weight thinking that would protect me, hoping he would not find me attractive. I abused myself with bad self-talk, and I always felt unworthy of any kind of love. However, I found myself still trying to please others so that they would like me. We were living on our boat, tiny quarters, and I kept running away until she would come home. So, she finally decided to get a small apartment for herself and my brother and me, and he stayed on the boat when she wasn't back at the house.

She never left him, just gave him a place to be when she wasn't home. I guess this worked out for them. By that time, I was a teenager and was always trying to find ways to protect myself from him. Between the drugs and the alcohol and the emotional eating, I was a mess. I still always did everything for everyone. As I got older, I began to ask questions and found out that my mother and her mother had also been abused by their stepfathers. This explained why they taught me to get over it and not talk about it. This was a pattern that was being passed on to generations.

When I was sixteen, I met the love of my life. He loved me for me and not for what I did for him. I really didn't think I was worthy of his respect. Three years later, we were married and started our own family, and we bought our first place with his mom after his dad passed away. After our first daughter was born, Myron was in a motorcycle accident and in the hospital for weeks, and then he was out of work for months.

We had just bought a new house and a new car, and we had a new baby. I was nineteen and dealing with so much. I had a breakdown. Myron's doctor saw me and suggested I start seeing his wife, who was a therapist. About a month in, I told her about the abuse by my stepfather. I had never told anyone except my mom about this. I was trained by my mom and my grandmother not to talk about anything and to get over it. They were teaching me how they had coped with the same abusive relationships with their own stepfathers. I knew this had to stop. I was determined that this wasn't going to be passed on to my daughters.

Over the next thirty years, we had raised three beautiful daughters and, yes, my mom and my stepfather were their grandparents. I told them both that he was never to be alone with my girls and he was to never think about touching them. I watched him and my girls like a hawk. He did apologize to my mom and me once over the years, but I still never trusted him.

I ended up telling my husband about the abuse about nine years after my therapy ended. Our oldest daughter was having some issues and I was afraid I had missed something. I think that because of her age I went back to my own feelings. This was the age that my personal abuse had started. My girls did not experience being abused; that was what I had worked so hard to make sure of. I told my girls about my own abuse when they were in their late teens. They each reacted differently. I knew that I had to give them the truth so that they could protect their own kids. It was so hard for me to share this information with my children, and my mom was not happy at all. And through it all, I still kept caring for everyone but myself.

By this time, my overeating had spilled over to my family. I was the one preparing the food. My husband who never had a weight problem was now also gaining weight. I saw my girls starting to eat because of emotions, just like me. They were taught these bad eating habits. I was the one doing the shopping and I was still a serious emotional eater.

I was more than one hundred pounds overweight and I felt

sick and tired all the time. Then, when my mother-in-law became ill, I stopped working to provide home-care for her. I took care of her for four years until her death. Then my mom got sick, and by the time she was seventy, doctors told her that they could not do anything more for her. I was fifty, and my stepfather was starting to show signs of Alzheimer's. He was being mean to me, and I told my mom that I would help her, but I could not care for him, too. She had to make a choice: if she wanted me to help her die, he had to go. I went to say goodbye to her, thinking he would stay with her, but I knew he could not care for her. I really believed she would choose him over me.

But his actions showed he only cared about himself. When the hospice nurse was sitting with my mom and me and he came home and asked her what was for dinner—that she needed to eat and so did he—that's when my mom made the call to his daughter and said to come and get him. There were eight kids, and all but three brothers decided that I had broken his marriage up. So, I began to tell them why I didn't trust him and what he had done to me. They all had a reason for believing that it was okay. My stepdad even wondered what my problem was because what he had done had happened over forty years ago.

Most of the family was verbally abusive to my husband and me, and then their neighbors were abusive towards us because he had to leave. My husband and I spent the whole month of May helping my mother die. Her husband never once called, not even just to chat or say I love you. I saw the pain he caused her, and that's when she told me not to let this ruin the rest of my life, that she had done the best she could with what she knew.

For a year after my mom died, I stayed in pain and continued to eat and drink and gain more and more weight. I just didn't care about me. My pain and sadness were driving everyone I cared for away. I was 51 years old and I couldn't see how great my life really was. I have a fantastic man in my life who always loved me no matter what I did to myself. I have three beautiful daughters who are strong and powerful women. I have four grandkids that I want to be around for.

I didn't want to lose my life, and the way I was treating myself, it wasn't looking good for my husband or me. Our health was failing fast. We decided it was time to change our lifestyle and put ourselves first for the first time ever. We began to make changes in our nutrition and then found that we needed to change our mindset also. We found ourselves that year with the help of a whole community of people and learned personal development through a company called Growth-U. We learned how the laws of focus help us advance through the cycle of growth. I began to learn that I didn't have to live with all the secrets, lies, and pain I had been taught to keep over my lifetime.

I was able to learn that I was letting my fear run the show. I started to see that my mom and my grandmother really did have the courage to get by in their own lives and did the best they could with what they knew. I was able to make sure that this pattern which had been passed on to three generations—the pattern of don't talk about it, get over it—had finally ended. I didn't even realize at the time how much courage it took for me to keep making sure that my girls would never know this kind of pain. I had never thought of myself as courageous, but now I see that my courage was passed down to me by those two women in my life who had suffered before me. I no longer blame them for not being there for me, and I am no longer a victim of my past.

For most of my life, I focused on what I did not want to happen. I watched my parents do the same, and we all kept getting what we didn't want. With the help of my amazing Growth-U family, I now focus on what I want out of life. This mindset has given me the ability to release over 100 pounds, and I can honestly say that I have knocked down those walls I had built around myself for over forty years. I no longer live with fear in charge of my life. I realized that once I stopped letting fear run the show, my courage showed up, and now my worries don't have a chance to run my life any longer. I get to choose to change the way I think and act. It's not as hard as fear wants us to believe it is.

I now know that, if something scares me, I am going to be able to grow through it and become stronger every time.

I really want everyone to know that it's never too late to live life out loud.

We don't have to let anyone else live rent-free in our heads. I now know that's what I did for most of my life. You are the most valuable asset you have. I finally realize I am worthy of so much love, laughter, health, and wealth in my life. I am the only one that can make sure I am living the life I designed.

It's been an incredible three-year journey getting to know myself, to love myself, and to understand that I get to choose how my day goes and how my life goes from here on.

At fifty-five, I am living life out loud for the first time, and I am watching my kids and my grandkids making better choices than I could when I was younger, decisions to make their own lives what they want them to be.

I hope my story will help some of you to realize that you have the power within to do, to be, and to have the life that you genuinely want. You just need to believe, love, and find gratitude for all that has ever happened which brought you to this moment in time. You get to decide how the future goes; you just have to grow through it.

I am so grateful that I get to live by the four laws of focus that my friend and mentor Rod Hairston has taught me:

What you focus on, you find;

What you focus on grows;

What you focus on seems real;

What you focus on, you ultimately become.

"You will never do anything in this
world
without courage it is the greatest
quality of the mind next to honor."

~ Aristotle

CHAPTER FIVE

THE LIFE OF DR. NEELU
A STORY OF COURAGE

By Neelu Parihar

Background

"Success is not final, failure is not fatal: it is the **courage** to continue that counts." - Winston Churchill

I believe that this adage perfectly sums up the story of my life. The more I think about courage, the more I find it to be my innate nature. Maybe it is a gift from my father. Or maybe it was an intimate mental response to my life's troubles. Whatever the case, I have always found courage as a close companion. This is the story of how I fostered courage through the various stages of my life, to the point of complete independence and unrivalled freedom.

My story starts with the experience of growing up with three siblings. Although an exciting journey, a welcome side-effect was that it taught me how to handle responsibility at an early age. The lessons in responsibility seemed to begin for me when my sister was born in 1995 and we realized after six or seven months that she could not hear us properly. A hearing disability was ultimately diagnosed, which was quite hard for the whole family, especially for my mother who loved her baby to the core and often had to travel across cities for my sister's health check-ups.

So, I took the weight of the household on my shoulders. At the age of ten, I learned how to cook, managed the household chores, and took care of my dad and siblings. As a result, I have an incredibly close connection with my youngest brother and sister to this day.

Considering my childhood, I believe I have had a lot of exposure to disability and how it can adversely affect the lives of the sufferers. That helped me to get sensitized to the woes of the special needs. We don't even realize how different their lives are from ours or the struggles they face just to get through a normal day. I recall a case where my cousin and her autistic child were abandoned by the child's dad after he succumbed to the pressures of parenting. I refused to accept the possibility of my sister having such a future. Sometimes when you don't have an option, you need to create one for yourself.

All of this motivated me to fight the world to make it a better place for her. This became an adventure, which also shaped my future along the way. I believe that my sister deserves to lead a normal life every day, just like you and me.

Eventually, I pursued a diploma in speech and hearing, which helped me to land my first job. This proved to be a turning point since I started working at the age of 17 while simultaneously working toward my graduation. My sister's disability played a big role in all these life decisions because I wanted to help make her situation better. Drunk with this fantasy, I ended up learning everything about the Oral/Aural technique to help her communicate better and interact with the world like the rest of us do. This eventually helped her to have a better social life, to complete two courses in Fashion Designing, and to land a job with Tommy Hilfiger in 2018. I will always reflect back to this milestone as the happiest moment of my life. Her dream today is to work with Louis Vuitton in Paris, and I intend to do everything in my power to make that dream come true.

Throughout my life, I have tried my best to learn all about my sister's condition so that I can help her to fight her limitations better. Today, I teach the Oral/Aural technique to as many patients as I can. But the limited application of the practice also motivated me to learn sign language. This additional skill helps me to work with completely deaf patients, especially children, to provide them with the futures their parents have envisioned for them.

Amongst all this, my father has been the perfect role model for me. As a professional wrestler, he has led a driven life, ripe of discipline and self-motivation. Today, even with a fracture in one hand, he shows up at the football field every morning and plays his heart out. In the evening, his usual wrestling routine follows. And he does all this at the age of 61! He will always be a mentor to me and has taught me the power of being fit and the importance of treating my body like a temple.

My relatives have always given me a hard time. I am a carefree spirit, and as experience tells us, such souls always have a hard time existing in the Indian society. I had to endure bouts of constant criticism regarding everything I did, whether it was the way I dressed or the friends I hung out with. Although this made me feel really low at times by stirring a bag of mixed emotions, it could never deter my self-esteem. In my heart, I was always aware that I was neither harming anybody nor doing anything wrong. The thought of proving myself to such people became a powerful trigger in my life and inspired me to be where I am today. So, whenever I recall that time, I just thank my relatives today for their criticism since it was the starting point of a rewarding life. Such challenging situations in life give you the courage to come out of your shell and aim for something that is bigger than yourself.

Also, I am grateful for the support of my parents. They never heeded the nonsensical advice of the world; instead, they empowered me to build a world of my own.

Now that I am an evolved person, in a way, I feel blessed to have such an extended family. If you see things from my perspective, they basically gave me more recognition than their own kids. Whatever I am today, I owe it to their attention and criticism. They helped me understand at an early age that, no matter what you do, the world exists to talk about you. You face it bravely and move on.

I have been let down by the world enough to understand that when you break, only you can pick up the pieces and put yourself together again.

Financial Acumen

"Money is not everything, but it definitely means a lot." These were the wise words of my mother. At a really early age, she made me understand the importance of money and how a financially independent woman can live life on her own terms. "It doesn't matter whether you use your independence or not, keeping your options open can never hurt you."

This newfound wisdom reverberated through my soul so profoundly that I bought my first house at the age of 23. People often tell me even now how crazy it is for a middle-class teenager to start investing in assets at such an early age, and I often reply with "Finance is nothing more than a belief system." I believe that anyone can be rich if he/she is courageous enough to develop an appetite for risk and learn to smartly manage it. It is a shame that in our country financial management is a skill that is mostly acquired by experience and seldom taught. Hence, you have to take the responsibility to teach yourself how to balance your financial life, which is always risky.

I overcame this risk by planning my life at an early age while I was still in Standard 10th. This led me to make some early investments and build a strong financial acumen in the process. It was also natural for me to develop a regular habit of saving. Eventually, I saved enough to afford the down payment for a second house and invested in a 10-year PPF scheme, which proved to be another great long-term investment tool for me.

The income from paying guests in the first house and the rent of the second house started a chain of investments into more properties. Ultimately, the rent from subsequent investment properties also contributed to the mix and finally gave me the financial standing I enjoy today.

This journey did not start out as a smooth one, though. My relatives tried their best to impose their financial opinions on me. Mutual funds were one of their top pieces of advice and I fell into their trap, not realizing that they were trying to rake in hefty commissions through my investment decisions. All this made me lose out on a small but important part of my corpus. But I do not regret it one bit since the experience provided me with a reliable know-how about personal finance. This acted as the stepping stone for my stable financial portfolio and made me realize the thrill of being autonomous with personal finances. As a result, this provided me with the courage to have more faith in my decisions.

One of the biggest financial learnings came during the time when I lent money to my relatives. This turned out to be one of the biggest mistakes of my life since it came with the harsh realization that money can ruin a loving relationship. One should never help another by directly providing them with the money they need. Instead, providing them the right knowledge or helping them learn a new skill is a much better course of action. Sympathy will not only ruin your relationship, but it will also make the person complacent towards solving their own life's issues.

I think all this can be summed up in a single sentence: Always invest with your mind, never with your heart.

My exciting career as a physiotherapist has also contributed to my life's success. I graduated as a Doctor in Physiotherapy in 2008 after a long stint of five and a half years in college. After a few years of job experience, I eventually went on to buy the franchise of a leading physiotherapy firm in a bid to understand the intricacies of the business. After three years of perpetual hard work, I finally mustered the courage to venture on my own, registered my company, and opened a Recovery Physiotherapy Clinic in Pune. Having no prior experience in business made this a daunting decision for me at first. The pressure of gathering every possible bit of knowledge about setting up and running an organization from scratch was enormous. But after a string of sleepless nights and constant hustles, everything worked out so well that I converted the business into a franchise.

Besides the investments and business I've built, I have recently ventured into the corporate world for the first time upon the recommendation of a friend. I accepted a business development role in Dubai that requires me to travel around the world. My friend was pivotal in making this happen by providing me with the right knowledge about the intricacies of the job as well as the interview process. Everything in this space was extremely intimidating for me, but he pulled me out of my comfort zone and constantly pushed me to try something new. Within two months in this job, I got the opportunity to go to France as a part of a business trip. I eventually plan to explore the field for better business opportunities that cement my place in the global corporate stage.

Given my humble beginnings, it was a huge challenge to manage all of this on my own. I believe I owe my success to my innate nature for trying to learn new things all the time. I don't think that anyone can ever be self-sufficient. No one should EVER try to be so. The moment you believe that you have reached the state of omniscience is the moment your downfall begins.

However bleak your chances seem, giving up should never be an option. As the proverb puts it, "Fall Seven Times and Stand up Eight."

Travel Experiences

Although I have travelled the world and would love to explore that space in an exclusive chapter later, my experience of skydiving is one of the most courageous things I have ever undertaken. It simply trumps every adventure sport out there. Why did I do it? Simply because Google told me it is the most adventurous sport in the world. I just had to try it once!

Let me paint a compelling picture of what it feels like. Imagine being thousands of feet in the air in a plane that is climbing higher every second. It approaches the drop point within no time and your heart rate shoots up to the point that you can hear it in your head. Fellow skydivers start jumping and before you know it, it's your turn. As you approach the door, you can feel the wind's pressure. And a few moments later, you are free falling to the ground like a bird who has just lost her wings. Sounds scary, right? But it actually turned out to be the most amazing experience of my life. There is an exclusive mental kick attached to the activity, which you can only experience thousands of feet in the air. It feels like you have suddenly developed the ability to fly. And, as soon as you hit the ground, every fear vanishes into the mix.

Actually, when I think about it now, I realize how everything fits together like different pieces of an integral cog. Whether it is about overcoming life's challenges, taking up adventure sport activities such as skydiving, or venturing into your own business, there is one common factor in every equation: Courage. You face challenges and push yourself through them. Success gives you more courage and you develop a risk-taking ability.

Every life experience comes with its own set of lessons. Life's struggles taught me the importance of being a responsible individual. Business taught me how to deal with risks and keep my head in high-pressure situations. And skydiving taught me that sometimes you have to jump out of a plane and fall to the ground in order to fly.

Marriage

My marriage life is particularly interesting.

Since childhood, I have been clear about the fact that I did not want to marry in my community, as I found the guys really dominating. This did not fare well with my carefree nature. I had also witnessed the culture of polygamous marriages in my extended family which I did not approve of. Hence, such a clash of ideologies with my family's culture made it extremely difficult for me to divert from my cultural background and choose a marriage that is right for me. I found myself torn between honouring my family's decisions and following my heart.

But as soon as I mustered the courage to take the right decision for myself, another hurdle followed. My husband comes from an extremely orthodox cultural background. The thought of going against his family put him in a quandary about his decision to marry me. But I did not let it hold me back and I ended up proposing to him. Although he did not say yes at first, he suggested that we give it more time. It took him two years to commit to me, and we finally got married in 2007, four years after meeting. His family did not support the marriage at all and not a single family member was present. If you watch the marriage video today, you will only be able to see his friends.

Right after the marriage, I left for Mumbai to pursue my master's, an endeavor that spanned a year. In 2008, I got a job opportunity in Bangalore. Soon after that, I often found myself traveling for work. This made it extremely difficult to balance my personal life with my work life. Though incidentally, that was also the time when I made a lot of friends in the city who eventually became as close as family for me. I learned a good deal about life from them and this new-found exposure transformed me into a whole other person altogether. Even today, my friends are always with me as a strong pillar of support in both hard and happy times. My husband and I eventually settled in Pune where my husband ventured into his business and I started practicing my degree.

I believe that the best thing about my marriage is that we never impose anything on each other. It is like an amalgamation of two individual souls who have created a thriving symbiotic relationship to explore and evolve together. We have a strong bond and we trust each other as we trust ourselves. We are stable pillars of support for each other. He is a completely skill-oriented person with a work-hard play-hard ideology, and I believe in financial stability. I think that a perfect marriage has three strong foundations: physical satisfaction, emotional stability, and financial planning. As a couple, your job is to efficiently manage all three of these effectively. And that is what we have been successful in doing. We take every struggle head-on and overcome it together.

Although our love for each other is eternal, everything in life cannot always come with a shade of white. Temperamentally, we are quite different. It actually took me a lot of time to completely understand him, the way he processes emotions and the manner in which he handles his everyday life. He has a reserved personality and mine is completely outspoken. He has a practical mindset while I have an emotional one. And I also think that all this helps us to be a formidable team. Although he can be honestly critical at times, his nature helps me to consistently keep improving myself through the years.

I think no marriage is perfect. And it is not supposed to be. Real beauty lies in life's imperfections. At the end of the day, my husband's perfectionist nature ends up adding grace to my goals. We thoroughly support each other in every situation. Take the case of my business, for instance. I had no idea about the corporate world and it was a huge leap of faith for me. My husband extensively supported me at the time and shared his knowledge with me.

Taking the decision to marry him was one of the most courageous things I have done in life. But we strove hard to make it right and lifted each other in the process.

Conclusion

I am grateful for all the struggles that I have gone through in my life because, in one way or another, they have shaped me into the person I am today. Every time I have had to come out of my comfort zone, I have undergone a transition that is graceful in its own way. This has made me realize that courage is not just a response to survival instinct; it is the foundation of being that transformed individual that we all picture ourselves to be in our wildest dreams.

I picture my future to be full of adventures since I plan to travel the whole world with my husband and explore every possible culture, cuisine, and custom. At any given point in time, we have a handful of holidays planned. Whether it be a music festival to attend, a mountain to climb, an adventure to experience, or a dish to relish, we have every travel goal pictured in our minds.

I have finally learned to live in the moment and cherish life as it comes, without letting fear interfere with the grandeur of the present.

"Courage is what it takes to stand up
and speak.
Courage is also what it takes to sit
down and listen."

~ Winston Churchill

CHAPTER SIX

RAYS OF COURAGE

By Susan Campbell Nickels

"I will love the light for it shows me the way, yet I will endure the darkness because it shows me the stars."
- Og Mandino

At eighteen years old I was no stranger to finding strength in the face of pain and grief. After visiting my father at a Los Angeles hospital, my mother and I climbed into my neighbor Jack's car for him to drive us home. On our way to the car, Jack said to me, "Your father was the man of men." Only a few years prior, adults and children alike would show up from blocks away with projects they knew that only my dad could tackle. He was a wizard when it came to fixing anything, and I mean anything. If the garage door was open at our house, that meant he was available to help anyone who walked in. He never took a dime for sharing his knowledge and expertise. My father had a beautiful, kind, and warm spirit that attracted people to him unceasingly. He was the person who would lend a hand no matter how hard the task. I prayed for the strength to hold onto and embrace each lesson I was about to learn, each ray of glimmering light, each Ray of Courage.

I remember one day, while my dad was doing masonry work building a wall in our backyard, I ran outside to see if I could be of assistance. "Would you bring me the level?" he would ask.

I would hand him the level that was just out of his reach, and he would make me feel helpful. My dad went to the garage to get another tool, and I accidentally tripped over and broke the snap chalk line that we had set up. I started to cry, and ran into the bathroom, knowing that I had ruined his layout tool. He called to me and I opened the door and explained to him what had happened. He quickly embraced me. I do believe a tear came to his eye because he loved me so much.

He said, "Come with me," and then we proceeded back to our project where he calmly handed me the chalk line where it had snapped. He gestured for me to pull on the blue chalk-covered string. I had no idea there was more line in the chalk box. I looked up to see my dad with a huge smile. He looked at me and said, "There's more where that came from." We repositioned the chalk line and continued with our project. I was so happy that I didn't ruin his tool, and my heart was deeply touched by my father's lesson: that we should never jump to conclusions. Even at only eight years old, I loved my father's compassion and his calm demeanor.

My father was a man who shaped his own world. When he wanted tables for the living room, he made them. When he wanted a brick wall across the front of our house, he built it. When he wanted a wrought iron fence around the pool, he welded it. When he wanted bacon and eggs for breakfast, he cooked it. Dad was gifted with the use of his hands in so many ways.

I couldn't wait for him to get home from his workplace at QRS Sign Company each evening so I could sit on his lap, watch TV, or maybe go outside with him and water the yard. It didn't matter what he did, as long as I was near him, I was a happy little girl. He was my hero, he was my friend, he was my teacher, and he smelled good too! This is why I could not believe it when

my parents told me that he had a terminal illness. I was 14 years old and didn't even know what the word terminal meant.

"Are not the rays of tiny light bodies emitted from shining substances?"

- Isaac Newton

I was born in Downey, California in 1959, daughter of an electrical sign maker and a housewife. My parents had two children, my brother, the elder by almost two years, and myself. My father was raised of the Mormon religion and my mother, a "Holy Roller" Protestant. After they married, they denounced both religions and referred to the Bible as their guide to life and this is how they raised my brother and me.

My life journey began with my umbilical cord wrapped around my neck. Nuchal cord is not uncommon. I was a "blue baby," as my mother would refer to me. I wonder about the amount of oxygen that failed to reach my brain. Are we given a choice to live to start at birth?

Our cute and modest home was made possible by a monetary gift for the down payment from my father's parents. I was five years old and playing in the front yard of our sweet home in my yellow polka dot bikini when the teenage neighborhood boys decided to use the front yard as their driving range for golf practice. I was hit directly in the forehead with a golf ball from three houses down the street. Luckily, my brother found me, although he thought I was dead. I was unconscious, having suffered a concussion along with bleeding in my brain. The bleeding behind my eyes caused me to be blind as well. Eventually, my sight returned without surgery, but I was left with amnesia not knowing what happened. It was on a camping trip at Bass Lake, California where we went to play miniature golf that it all came rushing back to me. I remember my brother yelling to my parents, "She remembers! She remembers what happened!"

Shortly after, my father made the decision that it was time for our family to relocate. We moved to our house in Hacienda Heights where I started kindergarten and continued my education through high school. I had survived the cord around my neck and a golf ball to my head, but this next challenge in life would be intertwined with my heart and soul!

On this life-changing afternoon, my parents walked into my room together. This was an odd occurrence. I was lying on the bed in my chartreuse-painted room with hippie flowers cut out of plastic remnants from the QRS Sign Company. (My father made these flowers especially for me in our garage, where he spent countless hours crafting magnificent creations.) My choice of colors was bright yellow, orange, and green. A cheerful room for sunny me until that very day when I looked up to see my father and mother standing in front of me with a solemnness I had not witnessed before. They began to cry as they shared with me the life-changing news.

Hope, faith, and continuous prayer became my way of life as I reached in search of answers. I would not accept the revealing words from my parents as true, and I honestly believed it was a mistake that would never come to fruition. I felt that I must search for a cure, a religion, an answer. I must become the happiest prayer warrior and heal my dad. I was 14 years old, and I knew I could treat him through faith and love. My search for a church began as I had a desire to be closer to God. I visited several churches in the area. Lutheran, no!

Presbyterian, no! Catholic, no! How many churches must I attend to find where I belong? God help me!

I was on the soft dichondra grass lying nose-to-nose with my dog, Star. I shared everything with Star. She was my confidant and best friend. I loved that pup like I have no other, and we had no idea what would eventually come between us. I lost interest in school, and food became my comfort go-to. I was one of the fattest kids at my school. I was lucky when it came to the mandatory school weigh-in; the school nurse was a gem and asked me to come by after school to weigh so as not to be embarrassed or teased by the other children about the number on the scale. I had been given the nickname "Cannonball Campbell" and was often teased by my peers. I can easily recall the chanting of "Cannonball Campbell" at every recess while continuing to keep a smile on my face and laughing it off. I would walk home alone after school and sometimes cry to myself until I reached my smiling pup, Star.

"I may have been given a bad break, but I have an awful lot to live for. With all this, I consider myself the luckiest man on the face of the earth." - Lou Gehrig

ALS, also known as Lou Gehrig's disease, is considered a progressive disease, which affects the nerves in your brain and spinal cord that control your muscles. As your muscles get weaker, it becomes harder for you to walk, talk, eat, and breathe. Motor neurons in your brain and spinal cord break down and die. It took over a year for my father to be diagnosed with this dreadful disease. It is difficult for me to write, but it is a story I have to tell.

The first sign that my father had ALS was his inability to open a mayonnaise jar. A strong, handsome, talented Marine no longer had the strength to open a jar. First, one hand failed, and then the other, as his muscles slowly deteriorated. I will never forget the day that he was unable to button his own shirt. After struggling for what seemed like an eternity, he dropped both hands simultaneously and said, "I can't do this anymore." We cried together, and he sat down on the end of the bed to relax after giving his all to try to button his shirt. This was the beginning of the end. I was 16 years old.

To cope, I would go down to the field and smoke a couple of puffs off of a joint before Dad's feeding time. I'm almost positive my dad knew I was a bit high on something, as I would act like I was feeding a baby and zoom the food in on a spoon in his direction like an airplane with sound effects. We would laugh so hard, he couldn't even open his mouth, let alone eat. This was my way of escaping the pain, and I did not have the experience at that young age to hold on to my power. Thankfully, I quickly learned that lesson. I didn't know it at the time, but this was the beginning of my life as a caretaker/caregiver. He asked me to make a promise to him that I would take care of my mother after his death.

I kept my promise to my dad, even though I eventually lived nearly 300 miles away. I drove back and forth every other weekend after Mom had a stroke some years after Dad's death. She would never admit or accept that it was a stroke, but if it wasn't, it was some sort of horrible curse that left her unable to speak or eat solid foods for 16 years. Mom's tongue was paralyzed. We use our tongue to form our words and automatically push food into our throat. For my mom, this natural ability was gone with the exception of swallowing blended foods or anything with the consistency of applesauce.

Mom's mind was on point and her mobility was quite remarkable. While still living on her own, with fabulous, caring neighbors surrounding her, she managed to keep her independence until she tried to kill a sapling tree by using the removable trash can lid as a tool to push the tree down. This, in turn, catapulted her into the cement side yard, resulting in a broken hip. I brought her home to heal, and she remained five years under my care until her passing. I miss my mom.

When my mom was still alive, I fed my dad once a day to give her a break. My mom became an incredibly strong individual, but she would go to her room and cry while I was on meal duty. I was her relief and her release! Then, she'd get right back to it with her chin up and love in her heart!

My dad's strength of attitude became so powerful, it was suspiciously unfeasible. Bob (my dad) kept a remarkably positive mindset with just an occasional breakdown throughout the course of his illness. He courageously accepted the reality that another muscle had died within his quantum being. Therefore, he could no longer ______. Go ahead, fill in the blank. What a cruel way for a disease to take your life and your breath, slowly and with full cognition to the bitter end. Muscle by muscle, he began to fade away.

During my senior year, I went to school for only half a day because I had enough credits to graduate, and I had to get to my job at "Micky D's" by noon. Money and time were short, and I still can't believe how my mom made two meals for a family of four with a single can of tuna! Marilyn (my mom) was a miracle worker in so many ways as she worked day in and day out to provide comfort for my father. Being high school sweethearts, they truly loved each other. My brother and I were put on the back burner as this love/death story was unfolding between our parents.

I had to find a home for my pup Star, as my father wanted to be in a study at the Veterans Hospital and/or USC. We had to be in a controlled environment with an agreement to stop all currently administered vitamins and drugs, and no animals were permitted at the homes of the chosen test patient. "Can I get her back when they find a cure?", I asked inquisitively. My parents said, "Yes." Star died in what I considered her foster home while I was waiting for a cure that never came. This is very painful for me to recall to this very day. Star never adjusted to the change, and neither did I.

I can recall pushing my father down the long, sterile hallway of the Veteran's Hospital with rooms filled with immobile bodies. I tried not to look into the rooms, but the harder I tried not to look, the more I wanted to. Eventually, we made our way to the room with all of the other patients in the study, each at different stages of ALS. Let the measuring of the muscle deterioration begin.

To be completely transparent, being a caretaker can be extremely exhausting. One day I came home and flopped on my bed feeling so tired after being at school all morning and then going straight to work until 5:00pm. As soon as my head hit my pillow and my mind and body started to relax, I would hear my dad calling my name. I got upset and cranky. "Are you kidding me? What the heck does he want now?"

At this point, he had to wear a device that strapped around his body with an adjustable chin rest because he could no longer hold his head up. I begrudgingly got up to go see what in the world he wanted. He said, "Sue, can you please change the channel for me and raise my head up?" My mom had just finished feeding my father and forgot to move his head up to a comfortable TV-watching position. I quickly completed his request and went back to my room, closed the door, and burst into tears. I was riddled with guilt. Please forgive me, Dad.

As the time passed, fewer and fewer friends would show up to see him. Jack and Chuck, both great neighbors, never abandoned him or our family. So many people found it difficult to visit with us, as he was immobile and hard to understand once his speech had declined. Jack and Chuck would trade off weekends and come over to watch a football game with my dad. This was a big deal to my mother and I because it also gave us a break, and we knew my dad enjoyed it tremendously!

On June 7th, 1977, my father passed away at 49 years old. He was only in the hospital for six days before his passing, which is pretty incredible, considering he was completely paralyzed from the neck down for over two years. My mom went into his room to say goodbye, and then I went in. Jack waited in the hall, comforting each of us between goodbyes. I was the last to see him, and he could barely speak, although he had the strength to look me in the eye and say, "I love you."

"Rising genius always shoots out its rays from among the clouds, but these willl gradually

roll away and disappear as it ascends to its steady luster".

- Washington Irving

When my dad passed, I felt as if I had been betrayed by God. In fact, I no longer even believed in Him. If there were indeed a God, He would have responded to my cry, to my countless hours of pleading and prayers. The little girl inside me who has now become a young woman was asking, "Why?" Why have you taken my incredible father away?

Please tell me why. He did not deserve to die by this cruel and debilitating fate."

As I sat crossed legged on the front lawn, the tears kept rolling out of my eyes, down my face, and onto my neck. I sat motionless, sad and mad at the world. I was in disbelief. I heard a bike approaching on the sidewalk directly in front of me. It was Yvette, a little girl close to five years old who lived three houses down. She looked at me sitting motionless on the lawn and asked, "Why are you crying?" I belted out in a harsh voice, "My dad died!"

I realized immediately that I had made a horrible mistake. She quickly turned her bike around to head back to her house with her eyes as big as saucers and a terrified look on her face that I wish I could erase from my memory. I burst into uncontrollable crying, facing the realization of my actions at that moment. I knew good and well that five years of age was too young to hear about the death of my father. I said out loud to the sky, "I'm sorry, Yvette, I'm sorry." Then something miraculous happened—what I consider a real miracle. A voice came to me from far away. At first I thought it was my dad speaking to me, then again, I believe it was God! Or maybe it was both!

This is the message I was given that day: "Susan, you have a choice to live a positive and loving life, or you can be mad and unhappy with the world forever. I hope that you will follow your dad's example of living life to the fullest and keep a joyful spirit. It is a choice."

From that day forward, I chose to live my life and work hard at being joyful, just like "the man of men."

We have a choice to live joyfully. Selflessness and love are the leaders to positivity. Our words, our thoughts, along with our attitude have a direct effect on everyone around us. Love gives me courage. I hope that my story has touched you in some way. I have a close personal relationship with God, Source, Higher Power, whichever name you choose. I embrace life with each muscle of my being, and I have been fortunate to have traveled the world and not take for granted that our greatest wealth is our health. I appreciate all of the beauty and creatures that surround me and

I greet each precious day with love in my heart.

My greatest accomplishment in life has been raising two thoughtful, intelligent, and praiseworthy children that are true assets to this world. Janet and John have found equally fabulous souls to share their experiences with, which makes me feel very happy and blessed. I have an incredible number of lifelong friends, exceptional friends, and a very best friend in my husband. I have cultivated my friends, as I've realized the importance of connection and keeping people in my life who have been kind and have had a genuine interest in me. I've worked to stay confident and aware throughout my life, and I continue to evolve with personal development and excellent mentors. I experienced the real ALS challenge, and I am here to help and inspire anyone going through this or any similar situation.

Each lesson I have learned represents an individual Ray of Courage. Each bright light ray was a piece of wisdom under my belt. One after another the wisdom and life experiences created the full spectrum also known as "Rays of God" or crepuscular rays. Some were meant strictly for me and even more, I believe, for my father as he handled his fate like a "man of all men". With every Ray, a brighter light would shine from within his soul. Although his body was fading he continued to laugh and smile and keep his fabulous sense of humor. Shining bright each of the rays of light inter-whined with me together, forever! I now carry his legacy and share our light with the world. As I continue my life without my best friend, Dad. I tap into the magic he left me and appreciate each day in my physical body. Touch me and you may feel me. Hug me and you may embody me. Love me and you may never forget me, or my father. Robert Walton Campbell Thank you Dad! I love you! We have a choice and I choose LOVE!

"Courage is being
scare to death and
saddling up anyway."

~ John Wayne

CHAPTER SEVEN

Sink or Swim

By Haimchand Katwaroo

May 25: The plane touched down in Winnipeg, Manitoba. My parents and I were about to begin a new life in Canada. The temperature was about 13 degrees Celsius, but when you come from a country where the temperature rarely falls below 22 degrees, it felt like winter to me. When the doors opened, I had the first glimpse of my new home. The feelings I had at that moment were so intense that they are still with me today. One part of me felt like it was Christmas morning and the present I was unwrapping was Canada. Another part felt like I was in a horror movie and was about to open a door not knowing if a serial killer was on the other side.

We had about $21 Canadian in our pockets. My uncle gave us some money to help us get started, and we lived with him and his family for a few weeks. My father found a job about a week after we were in Canada, and my mom found a job about two weeks after we arrived. In those days, factory and manufacturing jobs were plentiful in Canada. Wages and working conditions were not great, but my parents endured. Mom had sewn back home but had to learn how not to stitch her fingers together on the new machines here. Dad told the company he had worked with machinery before, but his second day on the job, his apron got caught in the machinery and he almost ended up inside the machine.

About three weeks after our arrival, we moved into our own apartment: a one-bedroom plus den. My den barely fit my single bed. We had minimal furniture and even less money. But my parents still bought me my first bicycle. I learned to ride the bike a few weeks later, but not before running into a brick wall and getting one of my many physical scars from the incident. I was amazed that my parents spent one of their first paychecks to buy me a bike even though we had very little money.

Since it was almost the end of the school year, I did not go to school until September. My parents went to work at 7 a.m. and got back home around 6 p.m. It was both an incredibly exhilarating and frightening experience. I had just turned nine years old, and the world was mine to explore; all I had to do was put my neck into that guillotine and hope the blade did not fall. I slowly started walking around my neighborhood. The country was so different from where I was born, and the people were all different. I was a stranger in a strange land.

I spent the next three months by myself trying to make friends. Before I had arrived in Canada, I think I had seen maybe two white people. In Guyana, we lived on a farm, next-door to my paternal grandparents who still had five daughters and one son living with them. My uncles and aunts were like my brothers and sisters. My grandmother spoiled me. I could do no wrong. Amazingly, I have encountered very little animosity from any of my relatives over her favoritism. For the first few years in Canada, I used this upbringing as my lifejacket because I was drowning in loneliness. Even though my parents tried, they had so much going on as they tried to adjust to life in Canada. I did not want to burden them with more problems.

The adjustment to life in Canada was tough. Even the simplest things, such as which toothpaste to buy, what type of winter clothes to buy, or walking/driving in the snow, were new to us. I did not know anyone in my neighborhood, I did not have any brothers or sisters, and my parents were away working. For the first few days, I spent my time indoors watching TV for the first time in my life. Life in Guyana had been spent mostly outdoors, and I could only watch so much television. I would peep out of my apartment and watch the kids playing. I wondered what they would think of the brown kid who moved into the neighborhood and whether the natives would be friendly. As Canadians, we have this fear of getting lost in a large US city and ending up in some scary neighborhood. I had the same feeling about my new neighborhood.

After a few days, I made it to my front door. I sat against the door, watched the kids playing, and hoped that someone would come by and say hello. There were many kids in the neighborhood. I noticed that there was a girl about my age who lived right next-door to me. She and her brother kept mostly to themselves, but after a few days, we started to say hello. There was a little playground about 50 feet from our apartment, and I would watch as the kids played on the monkey bars or pushed each other on the swings. I envied their laughter and longed for that day when I might gain acceptance and become a real Canadian. When there was no one around, I would venture over to the playground by myself.

After a few weeks, I saw a few Jamaican boys playing on the playground. I was getting really bored just watching everyone play. One day, I decided that it was time for me to say hello.

I spent about 10 minutes inside my apartment working up the courage to go and say hello. These boys were the only other ethnic people I had seen in the neighborhood. One of the boys turned out to be the same age as me, and we became friends.

The superintendent of the building also had a son who was my age, and he became my first Canadian friend. He and his family were very nice people, and I started to learn about Canadians. I can still remember my first taste of chocolate chip cookies… and then his mother gave us orange juice with it! Yuck! Don't get me wrong, I love orange juice, and I love chocolate chip cookies, but I could not help thinking, "These Canadians have strange tastes." We will not talk about the day that I discovered peanut butter and jelly sandwiches with a cold glass of milk while watching Yogi Bear trying to steal picnic baskets.

The rest of my first summer in Canada was spent learning about my new environment. I managed to make a few friends, but there will always be some children who can be cruel. The more I ventured out, the more often I learned new words, words like Paki, Towelhead, Raghead, Jungle Bunny, Spik, and a few others. Some people are able just to ignore these names, but I was—and I am still—not built that way. Outwardly, I put on a brave face and tried to convince myself that it did not matter. Looking back, I now realize that it was excruciating for me, and this was something I was unable to verbalize to those around me because I felt ashamed.

There is no feeling like it when you are in a group of kids and one of them starts making fun of you because of your skin color. I would run through a series of emotions so strong it could be unbearable. Unfortunately, that first and most powerful emotion was shame, and while it was often followed by rage and a desire for revenge, I was not built that way. I would simply take my lumps, go home and lick my wounds like a hurt puppy.

My weekday routine was waking up at 7 a.m. to watch cartoons, *Captain Kangaroo, Sesame Street, and The Friendly Giant. These were terrific shows, and I used them as my guide to becoming a good Canadian. My parents usually left for work at 6 a.m., but my mom would make breakfast and leave it for me to warm up. I would spend a few hours watching TV and then venture out into this big, beautiful, scary world on the other side of my door trying to make some new friends.*

We had some family and friends in Winnipeg who tried to make me feel comfortable and welcome. The Guyanese community in Winnipeg was small, but they had many activities. On weekends, we either went to our family for dinner or to a party. One of my uncles was always very kind to me. Whenever he would visit, he would give me a few dollars of spending money. I don't think I have ever told him how much his kindness meant to me. Despite all of this, I felt very alone in the world, and it was far more than just the fact that I was an only child. I think I have spent my whole life trying to fit in and learn.

I did not know it at the time, but that summer was instrumental in developing the foundations of my life, both the good and the bad. My parents had uprooted my life and theirs to come to Canada in the belief that we could make a better life and I could get a good education. I often questioned the sanity of that decision. I went from living in a community surrounded by aunts, uncles, cousins, grandparents, and friends who I knew cared about me to a world where no one knew me and some ridiculed me because of the color of my skin. I spent many hours crying in my apartment, missing my family and friends in Guyana.

At nine years old, I had some tough life decisions to make. I could either buy into the vision that my parents had, or I could spend my time whining about the difficulty of my existence. I spent a great deal of time weighing the pros and cons of the circumstances of my life. I like to think that I made a choice to stay in Canada and pursue my dreams. Back in those days, the immigrant mentality was much different. Parents would tell their kids they had to learn to fit in. We were living in Canada, and it was up to us to learn about the culture, customs, and laws of the country. My parents came here to achieve a better life, and they believed that hard work and perseverance were the keys to success.

The start of the school year was much like the start of every other school year for most children: a bundle of nervous excitement. This year was different for me because I was going to have to learn in a new school, new system, new classmates, new culture, new foods, and new faces. It was indeed a challenge. I continued to make friends but always ran into people who taunted and teased me because of the color of my skin. There were very few kids of different ethnicities in my school and in my neighborhood. I had always been an A student, and while it was difficult, I managed to keep an A average still.

Our next family challenge was the winter. Officially winter starts on December 21 or 22. But in Winnipeg, the temperature drops below freezing in November, and we often get snow then, too.

By the time winter rolled around, I was tired of being cooped up in our apartment. My mom was very proud that she had purchased me a down winter jacket. She had learned that down jackets were the warmest, and she wanted me to have a good jacket. So, I spent the whole winter wearing a t-shirt and my down jacket and wondering why I felt so cold. From December to March of that winter, the temperature was between -12Celcius and -20Celcius. With the windchill, it was often -20 to -30. My parents walked an hour to work for the first two months of winter. My friend Gerry got a job delivering newspapers, and I was so bored after school, I would walk with him while he delivered his papers.

My first snowfall was surreal. It was like millions of small white butterflies floating down. That winter, we built snowmen and snow forts. When the snow piled up five or six feet high, we made snow tunnels. I was introduced to the concept of a face wash. This is when someone takes a handful of snow and rubs it in your face. Refreshing.

I also learned why you had to stay away from the yellow snow.

Over the next year, we adjusted to life in Canada. I started learning about hockey, football, baseball, and soccer. I tried to watch American football with my dad one time. I could almost see the incredible amount of complexity and strategy involved. My dad's response was, "a bunch of guys running around and falling down on top of each other."

We were getting used to Canadian foods. In Guyana, we had never eaten beef or pork (although I am sure that my dad had) and my mom had never cooked anything but West Indian foods. She started trying to cook me some Canadian food. We still laugh about the day that she proudly brought me the eggs that my uncle had shown her how to cook "Half Moon Down."

I spent the next summer learning my neighborhood and getting entrenched in Canadian life. My favorite uncle asked me to babysit his kids that summer. I would go over to his house around 5 p.m. and look after his kids until he came home around 10 or 11 p.m. I was 10, and the kids were about 18 months and four years. My younger cousin would not sleep unless I pushed him around on his little red truck. I really loved those kids. My uncle was an avid cricketer, and we would watch him play cricket every weekend. Shortly after that, I got bored watching and decided to learn how to do the scorekeeping. Cricket is a beautiful game, and many families would picnic in the park and watch their father, son, brother, uncle, or friend play. For me, I longed to learn the new games that I watched on TV.

My parents worked their butts off to save up money to buy a house. With some unexpected help from a distant relative, they were able to purchase a home. It was a three-bedroom bungalow in the north end of Winnipeg, about a 15-minute drive from our apartment. We took possession of the home in November, and I had to change schools in the middle of the school year. It was great that we had bought a house, but changing schools again was frightening. My new neighborhood was 90% Ukrainian, Polish, and Jewish. I had to start all over again trying to gain acceptance.

My first day was frightening but uneventful. One of my uncles gave me the best advice, and I highly recommend it to every Canadian immigrant. He said, "If you are going to live in this country, you have to learn to enjoy the winters." Seems like simple advice in a city that experiences snow for about five to six months of the year. My uncle bought me a pair of skates and a snowmobile suit and told me to learn to play in the snow.

I saw that my neighbor's son, Tommy, and his friends played street hockey in front of our house. I could watch them from my living room. Tommy was a year older than me, and he had one of the only street hockey nets in the area. After a few days of watching from indoors, I moved outdoors and gradually made my way closer to where the kids were playing so I could learn the rules. A few days later, I asked my dad to buy me a hockey stick. Back in those days, they still made straight blades. I had the only straight blade in the neighborhood, probably because it was the cheapest stick in the store. But it worked out well because I had no clue if I was a right-handed shot or left-handed shot.

I would sit on the street near where the kids played and wait. I was too scared to ask if I could play with them. However, I knew that one day, they would have an uneven number of guys, and they would have no choice but to ask me. After a few days, Sheldon came over and asked me if I wanted to play. He also had not been invited to play with the older boys. We started playing our own games, and soon we were playing with the older kids. Sheldon and I developed a good group of friends, and in a short period of time, we would have our own street hockey game. Tommy and I also became great friends. We would play street hockey for hours every day after school. Sheldon was a good skater, and I started going skating with him.

There was no money in our family budget for lessons, so I learned to skate by watching others. Since I was the new guy who could not skate and I had the snowsuit, I got the opportunity to be a goaltender. We played with a soft puck, called a sponge puck, but when the older kids fired shots at me, it still hurt.

It was here that I met the bullies who would harass me for the next five years of my life. We would spend hours skating on the outdoor rink until our feet were frozen. They felt like they were thawing out as we walked home. I never became a great skater, but I never gave up trying.

The neighbors behind me had two boys. Brian was two or three years older than me, and Chris was one year older than me. Chris and Brian delivered a local newspaper called *The Winnipeg Free Press*. I found out that there was a job that was going to be open in a few months, and I was lucky because Chris and Brian helped me to get a paper route. I delivered papers from age 10 to 15. Every day after school I would spend 90 minutes delivering my newspapers. It was a great source of money. My parents allowed me to have the paper route, but their rule was that I had to put 75% of my earnings into a savings account. I opened up my first bank account at age 10.

That year, I saw that one of the best and quickest ways to make friends was to play sports. As spring rolled around, everyone was talking about the baseball team. I asked my dad to buy me a baseball glove. That year, I tried out and made the team despite the jokes about my plastic glove. I started in right field, and we won the championship all with my plastic glove. That summer, I took some of the money from my newspaper route and bought a leather baseball glove.

I also started learning how to play soccer, basketball, and American/Canadian football. I fell in love with football and dreamed of playing for the local professional team. In Canada, each season has its sports. Spring is baseball and soccer; summer is baseball, lacrosse, and football; winter is hockey, basketball, and curling. I played most of the sports, but my favorites were football, basketball, and baseball. I was too afraid to try out for the tackle football team, but I played touch football almost every day during the spring, summer, and fall. We had a playground in front of my house, and I would organize road hockey, football, and baseball games.

We did not have central air conditioning at the house, so we always had the windows open. My dad loved his Indian, soca, and calypso music. While my friends and I were playing, Dad would have his music turned up loud, dancing in his underwear with the windows wide open. It was not a pretty sight.

Eventually, at some point, my mother would interrupt the games and make me go home and eat. It became a standing joke when my mother would call me to come home.

I became very good at football. There was one boy who challenged me to a game. He picked his teammate and gave me the youngest kid in the group as my teammate. We ended up kicking his butt, and he got angrier and angrier. Then he told me that his dad was the mayor of Winnipeg, and he was going to have my whole family deported. I went home and cried thinking he really could do that.

My parents had told me that if anyone in our family got into any trouble with the police, they would deport our whole family. My parents were god-fearing, law-abiding people. After I calmed down, I went over to Tommy's house and asked him if what the boy had told me was true. He said to me that the boy's father was not the mayor and not to worry. I was still worried for the next week or two thinking that the police would bust down our door at any time.

Shortly after that time, I watched a mini-series called *Attack on Terror: The FBI vs. the Ku Klux Klan*. Great series, but maybe not what a 10-year-old boy should have watched. I did not understand the difference between the U.S. South and our little city in the middle of Canada. I honestly believed that this could happen to me. If I walked down the street by myself, I was afraid that a bunch of rednecks might pull up in a truck and kidnap me.

It did not help that two boys would call me names and threaten me every time they saw me. These guys used to chase me almost every day after school. Luckily, I was fast, but I always had my head on a swivel. My friends were all scared of them, and the boys were about two years older than me. There were many times when I daydreamed about taking a baseball bat and attacking them. But for some reason, I was too scared to tell anyone about it. I also found out that these boys had thrown one of my friends over a fence and had broken his arm. My friend was the son of a vice principal in our school. I thought, "If they can do that to him, what would they do to me?" Sadly, I was never courageous enough to stand up to them. This created a great deal of fear and paranoia for me that has lasted most of my life.

Middle school goes from Grade 7 to Grade 9. My first year was exciting but filled with anxiety and fear, as the bullies were also going to that school. In each grade, I set high targets for myself, and I measured myself against the best kids in each area—academic was David L; sports was Kenny P; social was Tommy K—but I also set small lower, more achievable targets. In Grade 7, I just wanted to make the basketball, baseball, and track and field teams. For each activity, I tried to learn as much as I could about the sport and then how to train to become better. I set up chairs in my basement so that I could practice dribbling around them. Academically, I was lucky; I had a great memory and understood the concepts. I paid attention in class and did my reading assignments and homework. I rarely studied hard, but I still got As and B-pluses.

Since my first year in Canada, I suffered from fear, anxiety, and panic. At first, I was very excited to have the opportunity to live in Canada, but over that first year, my fears overtook that excitement. As far back as I can remember, I have always had an insatiable curiosity about the world bundled with fear and anxiety. I wanted to see the world and to understand how things and people work. But I have also been extremely fearful of not being smart enough to understand everything or of making mistakes and failing. I believe in that old adage, "You can do anything when you put your mind to it." But I was always scared that it did not work that way in real life. The juxtaposition of these two thought processes has made me into the person that I am today: both daring and fearful.

By the time I started Grade 7, I had suffered from nightmares. Not the ghosts or goblins, but real-life nightmares such as failing a test or having classmates make fun of me or getting rejected by the girl that I liked. Those nightmares felt so real that I would wake up every morning for the next five or six years in fear of all the bad things that would happen to me that day. I would spend the first 10 minutes of my morning telling myself that everything was going to be okay and that my worst fears would probably not become a reality that day. I would have to beat back that fear and replace it with my goals for the day, week, or month.

In Grades 7 and 8, two or three bullies chased me almost every day and hurled racist insults at me. It was always the same three guys that I mentioned earlier. They only caught me once or twice, and I managed to escape any real damage. Looking back, I don't know that they ever intended to do any actual harm to me, but I was always afraid of the worst. I don't know if I just felt ashamed that I could not defend myself or if I was afraid that I would tell someone and they would not care to do anything about it. These guys made me afraid of venturing out and making new friends, and I became extremely self-conscious of the fact that I was very different from most of the other kids. Despite all of this, I did my best to enjoy my life.

Grade 9 was excellent because the bullies were gone and we were the oldest kids in the school. My morning panic attacks continued, but at least I did not have to deal with so many bullies. High school started in Grade 10, and I moved to a different school. Being new to the school and having to deal with all the older kids was challenging. The original bullies did not go to that school, but they were replaced with a few new ones. Although I did find some courage to stand up for myself a bit more, I still suffered from panic attacks. By this time, I had developed a good group of friends but still felt alone. Despite this, high school was one of the best times of my life. I loved meeting the new kids, playing sports, or just hanging around the 7-Eleven drinking Slurpees. Fear and panic were still woven into the fabric of my life, but I coped as best as I could.

If you are reading this chapter expecting to hear that I was able to discover the secret to courage and that I am able to sum it up in a few simple sentences, you are going to be disappointed. My life is still very much a work in progress, and learning how to manage and cope with the scars and pain that I have endured in my life is an ongoing effort. The most important things that I have learned are that all of this begins with hard work, sacrifice, and a willingness to accept your mistakes and learn from them.

I mention my scars and pain. I do not mean to say that my life has been so complicated. With time and perspective, I have come to realize that, relatively speaking, my life was not that difficult. However, whether you are a multimillionaire or just an average guy, many of us magnify our problems exponentially. I discovered this by talking to many of the people that I grew up with. I had thought the Canadian-born kids had it so easy. Once I heard their stories, I began to understand that they often faced many problems, and some viewed their lives as difficult or sometimes even more than I viewed mine.

Racism is a very hot topic in our society today. I have a great deal of personal experience with racism since I was raised before the existing anti-bullying rules that schools now have in place. Looking back, I did face a great deal of racism, but it was mostly from a tiny segment of the people that I met. I would put the number at less than 2% of the people that I came into contact with. Over the years, I have re-connected with many classmates through social media. Most were shocked to know that I had faced racism because they just saw me as "Haimer," not the brown guy. Even some of the guys that did call me names have told me that it was really more about getting under my skin than about the color of my skin. Once again, it was my own perception, fears, and anxiety that exacerbated the issue.

My transformational change came when I realized that the problems that I faced as a child were difficult, but it was more of the way that I reacted to those difficult situations made the problems worse. My fear drove me to panic whenever I encountered a difficult situation. In cases where I acted like the victim, the perpetrators of the bullying continued relentlessly. However, in those instances where I did stand up for myself, the bullies quickly understood and changed their behavior.

In my middle school, there was a speech writing contest every year for every grade. Ms. Nancy Charnley—the greatest French and Language Arts teacher ever—was in charge of the Language Arts class for Grade 8. My speech that year was about the racism that I had faced from some of my classmates. It was not the best speech or delivery, and I ended up with tears in my eyes and felt embarrassed. However, shortly after that, I noticed that many of the guys had stopped calling me names. In speaking to them years later, I learned that most of them really had not thought about how severely their treatment had impacted me. The lesson I learned from this was, if you continue to play the role of the victim, you will never have a chance to change your life.

Developing the courage to overcome your fears is the key to changing your life.

I do hope that my story will help others understand it is okay to have fears, and it is okay to be afraid. The best that you can do is to keep trying every day. That takes courage.

"Be brave, fight for
what you believe in
and make your dreams
you're reality."

~ Jared Leto

CHAPTER EIGHT

FINDING THE COURAGE TO BE MY AUTHENTIC SELF

By Theresa Rodriguez

I spent my life until age 13 in the low country of SC. I was a bubbly, happy, free-spirited child who stayed barefoot and dirty most days. We spent our days playing in the woods and swimming in rivers, always outdoors in nature. Despite my environment, I was a happy kid who loved everyone. I was also the child who asked too many questions, the child who couldn't sit still. I was called crazy, sensitive, over-emotional, amongst other things.

I rebelled against injustice and authority very early on. I always felt so misunderstood and was made to feel so different from others that I never thought I fit in or was accepted. I could never understand why people are so mean to each other or why people hurt each other for no reason.

I spent much of my childhood in a dysfunctional, unhealthy home environment. I was abused mentally and emotionally for many years. I knew it wasn't okay but felt powerless to stop it. I was always a highly intuitive person with a much greater understanding of things than most of the people I knew then. I was still seeking truth, knowledge, answers. I was the kid with never-ending questions. I wanted to know how everything worked. I wanted to talk about out-of-this-world ideas. This created many problems with my family, my teachers, and even at church. I come from a place where kids are to be seen and not heard, do what they are told, and grow up, go to college, get married, have kids, buy a house, and live the same day over and over like we were taught to do.

Then, at age 13, I was taken from my home and placed into foster care. This was such a life-changing event for me. I did fall victim to the system, and I was further abused and mistreated. Out of all my time in foster care and all the different homes I was placed in, I had one foster mom who truly made a difference in my life. I learned many valuable lessons during that time. I knew what a loving home was for the first time in my life. I had stability there. Then, I did end up living with my mom again when I was 16, but it was such a difficult transition. I felt like I had been raising myself so many years that I no longer needed her. I was working and taking care of myself already.

I spent the next few years trying to build a family from the chaos that I was brought up in. I went against my instincts and gut feeling day after day as I tried to fit into what society said I should be. But to be the mom, woman, worker, student, daughter, sister that everybody expected me to be meant suppressing and hiding my Authentic Self. It meant pretending to be someone I was not, and I did this out of fear—fear of judgment, losing everything, things not working, not fitting in, not being enough. I tried to make everyone happy and be what everyone needed me to be. I could not seem to find the courage just to be me!

By age 28, I had spent six years educating myself, hiding who I really was from everyone while going down some rabbit holes, changing my environment and the people in it because they didn't understand me. I even went back to college to study psychology so that I could understand myself, my husband, and my children. I intended to help us grow and to provide a healthy, safe environment in which our children could grow into their authentic selves without fear of judgment. I had been talking with my husband for months about mindset and change.

The more I learned about the world we lived in, the more I wanted to create change in our lives. I wasn't happy with living the way we were told to live. Each night my husband and I talked about our goals and dreams together. We wanted more. So, we started making changes with the new information we had. The problem for me was, everything I believed in and attempted to do went against what most everyone else thought to be right.

We were eating organic foods and cutting toxic, unhealthy foods out of our diets. Many family members felt that it wasn't just wrong, but was abusive, to deny children candy, sodas, and junk. We didn't make our children go to church or accept religion, either. Well, that really didn't go over well at all. Now we were going to hell and taking our children with us. We chose to homeschool/unschool our children, giving them freedom of choice in many areas of their lives.

Well, that really did it. We were told over and over by many different family members that we were cheating our children of an education. I was asked many times how I thought that I could give my children a better education than public school and then was told I could never teach them everything they would need to learn. We stopped the use of pharmaceutical medications unless absolutely necessary. We took our kids for survival training and instructed them to use weapons safely.

We knew that most of the people in our families did not understand or agree with the decisions we were making, but we never thought that they would go to the extremes that they did to try to force us to live the way they thought we should.

Our families were not as open-minded to change as we had hoped. We tried sharing information to help them understand our decisions, but they were not interested in learning anything new. We were put down, made fun of, and laughed at. We were ridiculed over our healthcare choices and even had several calls made by the family to social services because we homeschooled, refused to medicate our children, and didn't take them to church.

We were so confused and hurt. We could not believe what was happening. I spent many nights crying, feeling angry, scared, and alone. I was trying to stay happy and healthy for my family, but mentally I was depleted. Because of the calls, social workers had to come and talk with my children to close each case. Every time they called, a worker had to come out. This was traumatizing to our kids. They came out three times in two months. We tried to get restraining orders and couldn't without police reports. One caseworker who came out was just as appalled by the claims as we were. She thought what we were doing was absolutely incredible and wished us luck. All calls were unfounded.

While we overcame these unfortunate situations, they had really changed things within our family. We found ourselves feeling alone and under attack. Then there was a call made to mental health services by a family member who was angry when we cut her out. This person questioned my mental stability due to what she called irrational decisions I was making. This was proven to be false, but again my family was affected by the intrusion. My then-toddler was there when I had to go for the evaluation. She was scared and crying. Things were cleared up within a few hours, but at this point, I was so angry. I couldn't understand why this person wanted to hurt us so badly.

There was so much toxicity in our families that we could not see them. They were horribly controlling and thrived off drama. I couldn't understand how the system could put me and my family through this based on the word of one person, a person who had no contact with me at all. I found out that day that this could happen to anyone. I could even do this to a stranger.

We were being stalked and harassed by several family members during this time as well. We were being followed. We caught them going through our trash, and they would stop in front of our house and yell threats to our children about having them taken away. They threatened to use violence against us. It continued for months and we were exhausted. The system was failing to protect my children and our family. If an officer didn't catch them there, I couldn't get a report. I couldn't get any help from anyone.

I remember a conversation with my husband when we were talking about how damaging and unhealthy it was that the people we thought would understand and respect our choices were now a threat to our family. Our kids were scared. We felt so alone and lived in fear, unsure of what would happen next. We felt like we couldn't trust anyone anymore. We'd had enough, and we were burnt out. We had to do something.

So, we packed up our kids, took the last few dollars we had in savings, and left our home for a few weeks. We headed to the beach; we just wanted to give the kids a break and take time to focus on what we were going to do. We wanted to feel safe for a little while and clear our heads. It was hard not to worry about the bills, about my husband's job, about everything else that was happening. The first two days were spent just winding down and trying to relax. I knew we had to do something. I knew we had to do it together.

So, by day three, we were spending our free time each day reading more about the law of attraction. We spent the rest of the week working on changing our mindset and making different choices. We let go on that trip and let our authentic selves shine. We spent most of our cash out there and came back so that my husband could get back to work and we could start working towards our plan. We may have come home with no money, but the knowledge we had gained was higher than any dollar amount. We connected differently that week: the two of us sitting on the beach learning what it meant to live in the moment and to be grateful for our current situation. We were coming to an understanding that we could change what we brought into our lives going forward.

We headed home with a new mindset and ready to make our dreams a reality. We got home that Sunday to a disconnect notice for our water service. It was $90, and we only had $30 for gas to get my husband back and forth to work for the week. We got a little worried at first, and then I started breathing and remembering what we had been learning all week. I looked at my husband and said, "It will be okay. We will go in the morning and I will handle it." I spent the rest of the afternoon in peace, knowing that it would work out.

The next morning, we headed to the water company. I remember so clearly looking at the sky and knowing that it would be okay. Things were working out for us. I knew that they didn't take partial payments and that we were already on an extension for what we owed, but I felt like I needed to go and find out if I had any options. Forty-five minutes and one supervisor later, I had the arrangement to pay and only needed $60. Now that I was only $30 short, I remembered a pay card we had from a few months before. I was pretty sure I had $5 left on it. I was looking for any solution.

I had to enter the number twice and almost gave up, so when the automated voice told me that my balance was $37, I felt hot all over. See, the number 37 is symbolic to me. My husband told me when we were dating that I couldn't weigh more than thirty-seven pounds, and he nicknamed me 37 and even had me saved that way in his phone for years. It was engraved as my name on a gift he got for me one year. Thirty-seven dollars was the deposit amount. I had to hit *repeat twice to confirm it was really there before I believed it. It was actually there, and I wanted to know why. I called the pay card company and they told me it was a reversal of a payment, but they couldn't see the amount made. We never really cleared it up, and we never found out where it really came from. I had never made a payment.*

I ran back into the water company and paid the amount owed and only had $7 left over for gas. It wasn't enough, but I felt even more confident now that it would work out and be okay. As we pulled out of the water company parking lot, I noticed a towing company across the street. It looked a lot nicer than the one that my husband worked for, so I encouraged him to stop in and apply. He came out with a new job starting the next day, making a lot more money and with a lot more opportunity. The best part: the $7 would be enough gas to get him back the next day when they would give him a truck to drive home at night on call. This changed everything. I knew at that moment that changing the way I thought was going to improve our lives. We spent the next two years working hard towards building a better life.

We were always working hard to do the right thing. We had cut out the toxic people. We were buying a house, and I was a stay-at-home mom. We were living a healthy lifestyle, and my husband worked overtime every week, trading his time for money so that I could homeschool our children and we could afford healthy foods and to vacation every year. We were always told how happy we should be.

The thing is, this wasn't what we really wanted. We wanted more time together, more experience, fewer things. We wanted to travel together and live a minimal life. It had taken courage to make the changes with our education choices, our food choices, and our healthcare choices, but what we were about to do would require courage that we didn't know we had at the time. I remember sitting there—in the moment— indeed surrounded by nature. The kids were laughing and playing nearby in one of our favorite little swimming places. We loved being there, to disconnect from everything. I had put so much time and energy into learning what I needed to make the best choices for our family. I was there in that moment, that day, to find clarity. I had big decisions to make.

After having learned so much, being hurt so much, and overcoming so much, I kept asking myself – how? How do you live the way that everyone says to live when it's not how you want to live? We'd talked so much about traveling after the kids were older. Why wait?

By the time my husband got home from work, I had a plan laid out on my whiteboard. I had worked out all of the numbers and figured out how we could live more freely, work less, have more, and go anywhere we wanted to. We could sell our house, buy an RV, and minimize. At first, all I got was a crazy look, but then we spent hours talking, planning, and coming to the realization that traveling and genuinely living with our children fit more with our goals and life plans than what we had been doing. We already homeschooled, so school wasn't an issue. We talked to our children and included them in the decision. Together, as a family, we decided to go for it.

We spent months researching, joining groups on Facebook, looking at options, and planning. We kept it quiet out of fear from all that we had been put through before. After months of planning, we reached our deadline. While making our final preparations, we started to get anxious, doubting what we knew was best. We questioned ourselves and, as a family, discussed the risks involved. The people I had trusted most had turned on us before—for things I knew they would consider much smaller issues. These lifestyle choices could be seen as extreme by some. What would people say? How would they react? We knew we wouldn't be accepted or supported by everyone, but we knew we had to have the courage to go for it.

We couldn't stop now; we had come too far. What could they do to us? We couldn't care anymore. We bought the RV. We packed up everything we were keeping, sold the rest, and sold the house. I literally drove off into the sunset with the freest feeling I had ever had as an adult. We were free to go where we wanted and to live life by our terms.

Of course, people did really think we had lost our minds at this point. Many calls were made. We didn't care. We kept living, stayed true to ourselves, and overcame every obstacle in our way.

We were in control now. We were empowered, healthy, and no longer living in fear. We are now living the best versions of ourselves while continuing to learn and grow. We still face challenges and hit bumps in the road, but we have learned to deal with these problems differently. It still sometimes scares me to think about what our lives would look like if we hadn't dared to stand against our family, the system, and the programmed thoughts to live our lives the way we wanted to. We were faced with so many challenges where we had to find the courage to face our fears and rise above them. We learned to step outside our comfort zones, to persevere and keep creating the life we want while releasing the harmful, toxic energy. We can't let fear overcome our courage. Having the courage to stand up for our true selves led us to be our most FREE selves.

"Sometimes all you need is
20 seconds of insane courage.
20 seconds of embarrassing
bravery."

~ Unknown

CHAPTER NINE

THE COURAGE TO MOVE

By Donna Pearl

One day in February of 2013, I found myself pulling up carrots and beets from my aunt's garden in Tallahassee, Florida. The soil was warm, rich, black, and fertile. I had been in Tallahassee taking care of the affairs of my late father's estate. He died on January 23rd of that year, which also happened to be my youngest grandson's fifth birthday a day that he and I will both remember, vividly. He saw me broken down and sobbing on the carpeted floor of my bedroom. He had come down to my apartment from his third-floor dwelling where he lived with his mom, my eldest daughter, Ebony. I'm sure it was a frightening sight for him to behold.

I loved my dad with all my heart. We were very close. As a matter of fact, he had called me the Friday before he died to tell me that he was taking me up on my offer to come live with me in the southeastern region of Boston in a city named Brockton, Massachusetts. Brockton seemed so far away on that February day, as I pulled up those root vegetables. My friend and spiritual mentor, Jill Wiley, said that pulling up those beets and carrots from the very soil that my great-great-grandfather tilled was very symbolic of my feelings of being called to this place. That symbolism would grow ever more clear, as I realized that I could get used to this life, this weather, and this place, so different from cold, snowy

Massachusetts. The land that I was on was purchased by my great-great-grandfather, Prince Griffin, post-Civil War at a time when formerly enslaved individuals, who were blessed to be able to, began to stake their claim where they were now deemed free by the Emancipation Proclamation. To this day, the land remains in his name due to a long, drawn-out probate battle between his surviving family members, my mom being one of them.

We spent many a summer in Tallahassee. My parents would drive my siblings and me down to spend two weeks visiting with relatives that called the area home. My parents were both born and raised in this area. My dad was from Midway, a town about ten miles west of Tallahassee in Gadsden County. My mom was born in Tallahassee and was primarily raised on the very land where I found myself standing on that day. My maternal grandmother, Joe Ella, was the steward of that land for decades, as her siblings really didn't want anything to do with it. She and her only brother lived on what was left. Contrary to what some may think, my grand uncle Bubba wanted her to lose the land after she had refused to sell her share. Her cousins sold their 40 acres in the early 1960s for approximately $2000, such a small pittance that must have seemed like a boon to them at the time.

However, my grandmother kept her portion and took on menial jobs to sustain herself and her family, like doing laundry, cleaning and cooking for neighboring white folks to pay the taxes, insurance… basically eking out a living from the remaining half of the 80 acres of farmland that Prince Griffin received in trade for 120 acres that he originally owned in town.

Even though I had never lived there, I immediately felt like I belonged there from the strange sense of peace that came over me. Having grown up in Springfield, Massachusetts, educated, and currently living in the Boston area, I had never felt the same feeling in my bones as I had when I was in Tallahassee. It was odd yet quite delightful at the same time!

Briefly, during my junior year of high school, I contemplated attending college; there. I had even told my grandmother that. I am sure that she was deeply disappointed when I told her that I would not be moving to Tallahassee to go to school. It wasn't my time. However, I can feel her pain now that I'm a grandmother; myself.

After spending six weeks there post my father's passing, I returned home with a plan. I was going to put my house on a short sale and move to Tallahassee, once the house was sold. That journey back home sent me on a strange odyssey. It started with a trip to Las Vegas, one of the places that I loved to take my mom and aunt because they liked to gamble and I loved to travel. We established an annual trip there in 2007 when I'd received a settlement from a previous employer. Little did I know that would be our last annual trip to Vegas.

Upon returning from Massachusetts by way of Las Vegas, I put my three-family house up for sale. It sold in 11 days, but the actual closing would not take place for another year. Don't let anyone tell you that a short sale is quick. According to all realtors that I spoke with, including my best friend Shirley, short sales take a long time to close. In the meantime, my daughters, my grandchildren, and I remained living in the building that I had purchased in 2004 after divorcing my husband of 19 years.

At the time, I was living on my retirement savings and working full-time as a non-profit director of a theater company that I founded in 2005 and incorporated in 2011. Those were heady days for me. I was doing lots of creative performances and festivals for Indaba Theatre. I loved the freedom and flexibility of calling my own shots and expanding my role as a writer, producer, director, performer, organizer, event planner, and all-around administrative hack for my passion. Indaba Theatre's mission is: "To inspire, empower, uplift, and create healthy outlets of self-expression using theater as therapy to help people overcome obstacles in their life." A mission that I would soon realize that I embodied in my daily life and practice.

At the time, my desire to move to Tallahassee was unclear to me. I just knew that in my bones, I had to go. I had to be there for whatever the spirit was that was leading me there. Initially, I thought I was being led there to live in and take care of my father's house. It was a home that he had custom built on land that had been purchased by his mother before she passed away in 1958. My dad served in the Air Force for 25 years. As a young man in the military, he would send his mother money as often as he could to help support the family. His father had passed when he was only 12 years old, leaving my grandma with 18 children to raise. He fathered 15 with her and she had three children from a previous marriage. My grandma's mom, Millie Bradwell, was a descendant of Mingo and Sarah Bradwell. In 1838, Mingo had been sold at auction to the Bradwell family at the tender age of eight years old. The Bradwells purchased about ten other slaves along with Mingo from an auction in Goose Creek, South Carolina. Mingo's mother was sold to a Bradwell brother that settled approximately 30 miles from where Mingo's owners eventually settled.

The Bradwell family moved to Bainbridge, Georgia and lived there for a time because of the massacres that were going on between the Natives, Whites and free Blacks during the second Seminole War. Sarah was a Native American girl that was saved from the Trail of Tears by enslaved women. When the master found out about her, he wanted to have her killed.

But those who had rescued her begged the master to allow her to stay. He acquiesced. She took on the name of the overseer and eventually married my great-great-grandfather, Mingo.

All of these issues of belonging and not belonging would appear in extraordinary ways once I moved to Tallahassee. When I arrived, I did not realize that I would be homeless and jobless, or how I would be scorned by those who didn't understand my purpose nor saw the vision of who I was becoming. As I grew into the new me, I would no longer allow shame, blame, and guilt to define me. My friend Karyn used to say that guilt was a wasted emotion. I can't count how many times her refrain saved me from turning back from my decision.

I would soon find out that being homeless and jobless was actually quite liberating and brought more blessings than I can count.

That summer and fall of 2013 brought more travel than usual. I was blessed with the opportunity to return to Tallahassee in July with my aunt and my Mom. They traveled there by way of my aunt's minivan to go to a court hearing to settle the estate of Prince Griffin - or so they thought. It turned into a tragicomedy that still has not been resolved. It was a drama that I was not expecting, after returning from a side trip to New Orleans. It was Essence Festival time in New Orleans, another favorite place and one of my favorite events of the year. Wow! That trip changed the trajectory of my life and my entire being. It took me on a path that led me to Bali, Jakarta, London, Johannesburg, Capetown, New Delhi, parts of southern India, then back to Bali and Jakarta.

Who would have thought that my father's death would bring on all of this? The beauty was that I felt my father's push every step of the way. Rarely a day goes by where I'm not grateful for my father's posthumous redirection of my life. It would take many a workshop and thousands of dollars to get here. But I am eternally thankful for the doors that he opened up for me to be on this incredible path.

During all of these peaks, there were also valleys. My friend Jill used to say "Remember, when you're walking in the shadow of the valley, there are great mountains beyond for which you will be able to see the view of what you have come through."

About those twists and turns... In New Orleans, I met a famed guru and life coach, Lisa Nichols. Through our chance meeting, I was invited to Bali to attend an exciting event called "Awesomeness Fest." My first Bali trip was a fantastic feat of manifestation, responsible for the book which I'm still writing today. What was really interesting was that while I was in Bali, post-Awesomeness Fest, I met a man from Tallahassee. Yes, Tallahassee! All the way across the world in Bali, Indonesia, I met and got to know this man named Angel. That was my first inkling that I must return to Tallahassee, and Angel had been put in my path to remind me of that.

Once I returned back to the United States from Indonesia, I immediately started writing my book and recording all of the amazing things that led me to Bali. However, when I returned from Bali, I had an invitation to go to South Africa! The land of Indaba! I was blessed with an invitation from an international drama therapy organization that wanted me to present on a performance that Indaba Theatre held for three years titled "Woven Stories of Love, Hope and Healing - From Silence to Joy for Survivors of Domestic Violence." It was another opportunity that I could not refuse. I scraped together whatever little monies that I had left to go there.

In the meantime, I had also been invited to a double workshop to present at in New Dehli with my new found friends from Awesomeness Fest. Since I was going to be so close, I decided that I would return to Bali to finish writing my book. I thought, 'What a journey! I'll finish my book in the land where it all started.' I also planned a side trip to Jakarta. I was invited to speak there as well by another Awesomeness Fest friend. My life had become like a fairytale to onlookers, but I was teetering on faith, courage, and following my destiny.

My destiny actually brought me to a crash in Bali. It was truly a low point. I, of course, did not see that coming and had not anticipated how crippling this trip would be, literally and figuratively. I had not been in Bali 24 hours before I ended up crashing a scooter and breaking my leg in three places. I had arrived there late, after missing my connecting flight in Malaysia. I got to my hotel cottage around 11:30 pm from India. When I got there, it was too late to purchase adapters for my electronics. I had forgotten to bring the ones that I got on my first trip. I needed them to power my tablet and phone while I was there.

The next day, I actually walked for about an hour in the hot sun to buy an adapter. I bought one that would screw into a light bulb. It was inexpensive and the only style available. When I got back to my room, I discovered that it would not fit in the lamp on the nightstand. A storm was approaching, so I decided to stay in and take a nap. Once I woke up, I went to the eatery at the place where I stayed and inquired about someone taking me in town to buy adapters. They suggested I take a scooter. I got what amounted to a ten-minute lesson, then off I went. I was able to return the adapter that I bought earlier, get to another location to buy a couple that would plug into a regular socket, then I set out for my final destination back to the cottage.

Lo and behold, I missed my turn and ended up going way out of my way. Once I realized it, I turned the scooter around and headed back the way that I had come from. Darkness was starting to fall and I knew that I had a turn coming up. (Mind you, I'm driving on the opposite side of the road.) I looked up to see the street sign ahead to my right and the turn was coming up on the left. As I torqued the engine to turn, the scooter took off straight into a clump of trees. I was moving quickly toward the trees and my spirit said, "This is not going to end well."

I ended up in the hospital for nine days with three fractures and nine screws in my right leg just below the knee. It was a heartbreaking experience and deeply humiliating. I could not understand why the spirit had allowed me to stray so far off my path. I learned a valuable lesson. Pay attention to your surroundings! In the meantime, I also learned that I had terrific new friends that I would have never met had it not been for Awesomeness Fest. They were my rock and my strength during the rest of my stay in Bali. My first visitor was John Spender, of all people! I actually ran into John on my trip to India. It was a very serendipitous occasion in New Delhi. I had only been there a couple of days, it was just before Christmas. I was in a hired car with my new Awesomeness Fest friends, Seema, Kamal, Kamal's soon-to-be girlfriend Wioletta, and one of my very best friends and publicists for my upcoming book, Nicola Simpson. Seema, Kamal, and I met John through a mutual friend while in Bali. Here we were, driving down a crowded street in New Delhi at dusk, and who steps into the road in front of us? John Spender! We all jumped out of the car and gave him big hugs. It was amazing and fortuitous. I had pondered whether

I would see John in India because I knew that we were both going to be in India at the same time.

John visited me quite a few times in the hospital, bringing me necessary personal care items and nutritious coconut water that helped ease my nausea. John also brought me to an orphanage on the very day that I was released from the hospital; which immediately took me out of my own misery and gave me empathy for others who had it much worse than me. I returned home to Massachusetts through a series of highs and lows, feeling somewhat defeated.

I had almost forgotten that I was supposed to be moving to Tallahassee. I came home on crutches still in need of rehabilitation. I did not know where my journey was taking me. I ended up in San Jose, California for a couple of months and contemplated moving there. But, I had to return to Massachusetts for a workshop that I was taking for Drama Therapy in Jamaica Plain and a conference that I was presenting at in Western Massachusetts, where I had grown up. The conference that I presented at brought me face to face with my destiny.

The day after my presentation, someone asked me where I was going. I was about to say, "Back to California." But, my spirit said, "Don't go back to California, stay in Tallahassee." As soon as I mentioned that I was going to Tallahassee for a family reunion, they said that a person who had taken my workshop the day before was from Tallahassee. At that moment, I knew that I had to follow my spirit.

It's been four years, now and I haven't looked back. Sometimes you have to blaze a trail for others to follow. Let your purpose propel you to leave a mark. Some may ask, what helped me be successful on this part of my journey. I found an outlet for my passion. I found my artist community,

I found my activist community, thereby giving me the space to create and continue to spread my wings. I set small goals like employment, housing and developed a network organically through church and work. I celebrated my small wins. I allowed myself to be happy, knowing that I had the freedom to change my circumstances if I so desired. Create your support system. My mom, my children and my best friend back home were my foundation that kept me strong.

Multiple elements are necessary to achieve success. So many things have happened on my path, that I no longer question why. I ask for clarity and divine revelation as affirmation. I look for the signs along the way. We wouldn't need a map if the road were straight with no hidden corners or driveways.

Be patient with yourself, step by step. As you walk this journey, take heart knowing that others before you faced similar challenges, yet overcame. I did not get my father's house, the very reason that I thought I was here. I have found and lost jobs, occupations, moved several times within Tallahassee in the last four years. But, yet I know that I am in the right place at the right time. Never lose track of your inner compass. My compass told me to pack my two carry on bags with $175 in my pocket and move to Tallahassee. I was blessed with a job and permanent housing within a month of following that calling. The darkest moments help you identify what the next necessary steps are on your journey. Facing down your nemesis is par for the course. Jesus had Judas. We will be tested on the path. Your test is your testimony.

I hope that all reading this understand that you have the power to heal your life! It is in the telling of our stories that we begin to heal. Determine to find what is holding you back. What makes you feel comfortable? What makes you feel like you're home? Identify deeply held ancestral beliefs, your native tongue and spiritual rituals that cleanse your soul.

My best advice to the reader is to love yourself through the journey. The top five things that I suggest are to:

1. Change the false narrative, listen to and trust your gut.

2. Have an accountability partner, someone that you have a tried and true friendship with. It could be a parent, a child, your spouse, a trusted friend, someone who will tell you the truth about yourself, even if it hurts.

3. Count the blessings, see the abundance in your life, even if you are in the shadow of the valley of doubt.

4. Don't beat yourself up. Don't "should" on yourself.

5. Do the mind work. Allow positive thoughts to stay with you. Be your best friend. Tell yourself the good things that you want to hear from you. Release negative energy.

Healing oneself mentally and physically is a lifelong journey. Do the things that you love. Don't wait for someone else to validate you by acknowledging your mere existence.

What's next for me? Through the gift of my current book that I'm writing, "That's My Bali," I am willing to dig deeper into my story. I have had so many revelations in the last six years. My gut tells me that there is a book and movie inside me. Throughout this journey, I have learned to trust my gut, no matter what! I will stand in my truth, free and clear of guilt, blame or shame. My work is never done. As long as I'm breathing and as long as I can move, I will continue to follow my purpose to inspire. Choose to live your life on purpose!

"It's never easy.
And it's never over
it will be a fight renewed
each morning but it's
possible!

~ Jamie Tworkowski

CHAPTER TEN

COURAGE IN EVERYDAY LIFE

By Alice Ho

"Think of your mind, your emotions and your spirit as the ultimate garden. The way to ensure a bountiful, nourishing harvest is to plant seeds like love, warmth, and appreciation, instead of seeds like disappointment, anger and fear."
~ Anthony Robbins

First things first, what is fear? As human beings, we all have doubt. When we are born, our parents say No to us, and when we are teenagers, they restrict us from doing things. As we grow up and face a lot of challenges in life, we learn to conquer our fears by accepting our flaws, by being creative and giving ourselves the freedom to be who we really are. Remember childhood. Every one of us had a dream. Our teachers and parents hoped for us to grow up to be successful in our careers and taught us to dream of what we would do with our lives. Sometimes, through life-challenging experiences, we almost forget what is essential and can't remember our dreams. But I am grateful for my parents who gave me a lot of freedom to choose what I loved to do. My father is a painter, and since I was young, I saw him paint many houses. And in our house, he painted a lot of color on the walls. I still remember that he liked to draw the Mickey Mouse character during my childhood. From the first moment he did this for me, I liked color and drawing. I love this quote from Walt Disney: **"All our dreams can come true if we dare to pursue them."**

What kept me holding on while going through a lot of challenging life experiences was the courage to chase my dreams, to choose love in an effort to understand others, and to be grateful for what I have. Eventually I realized that, as we age, we become more afraid of changes in our lives. For example, from changing jobs, changing career paths, and starting a family, all the life processes we go through require a lot of courage and faith.

In the current moment, I am going through the experience of changing careers, and I am really lost as to which path to take. I feel that I am going through the downside of my life and am not sure what is the next step to take. I'm worried and losing direction and do not know my purpose for the career or the job I'm doing. That is how I came to know Christ. God gave me faith and hope. He said he will take care of me and would provide the future I desire. I will share more on my career and work progress in my chapter.

Discovering my Inner Warrior

One day at a networking event a friend invited me to attend a free seminar. And during the seminar, my friend asked me to sign up for the course package. For me, the cost for their program was such a significant investment.

I was struggling and hesitated, unsure whether I wanted to buy the course or not. It took a lot of courage to sign up for the full package. After thinking twice, I decided to sign up for the entire program. For one of the courses, we needed to travel all the way to Malaysia. The venue was used as an army training camp. It was a fantastic place and such a good experience throughout. It was really encouraging and empowering and helped to break the behavior patterns that no longer served us.

One of the activities in training was to bend a steel rod using the center cord of the throat. How can our throats turn a steel rod? It was about 8mm thick! The thought crossed my mind that this will hurt, and I was so afraid to do it. The course taught us, to have the courage and do it.

Two people were needed to bend the rod. Each person placed the steel in the pit of his throat and the two walked towards each other. In about five minutes, I managed to bend the steel rod. What an amazing thing to witness and do! What I learned from this tough situation is that, when we face a new thing that is unfamiliar, we will be scared to do it in the beginning. But after working through an experience, we learn our limitations and get to know ourselves on a deeper level.

Eventually, there was one of the activities which I found took a lot of strength and perseverance. I carried a massive block while walking on the beach. I was tired and exhausted throughout the whole process. I had no energy to do this task. But, luckily, before attending this course, I had been in the habit of running for my weekly exercise. The challenge was carrying the block and walking more than 5km in the hot sun.

Through this, I learned to develop a persistent mindset and surrounding myself with a lot of positive people is critical. I also learned that we need a positive synergy, motivation, and purpose in life to carry us and we need to live every day to the fullest. For me, during the course, I was learning to be brave enough to speak out about my ideas and opinions in the corporate world, to be persistent and not to give up easily on something when starting out. I also learned the courage to ask questions and to speak confidently to all people, regardless of position or race. In the past, I would not dare to share my thoughts.

The Gift of Travel

Traveling is my hobby, and I like to see different cultures in other countries. I especially like traveling to Europe. The architecture and design and the history inspire me the most.

One of my friends was stationed for a month in Taiwan. One day, she asked me to join her. Grateful in my heart, I booked a ticket and flew to Taiwan by myself. I remember that it was winter. When the plane landed, I stepped into this beautiful city of Taipei, Taiwan. I was excited to explore new cities. Before, I was worried about my finances. But, thank God, my friend invited me to stay in her business hotel room.

Since my friend was working during the daytime, most of the time I was exploring the places by myself. I tried to make friends with the local people. I had a list of places to go. Excited, I was meeting a couple on the train. They were from Singapore. Such coincidence, we were traveling to the same place: Pingxi! This is the place where people write wishes on paper lanterns and release them into the sky with the hope that their ancestors will answer their prayers. The countryside is scenic and the perfect place to experience making your own lantern and releasing it into the atmosphere. I was excited to make new friends in Taipei. This was the first country I visited on my own. It was the trip of a lifetime! Everyone should experience it. I needed a lot of courage to travel on my own, and what I learned was how to enjoy myself and to just be myself.

After a few years, I had a chance to visit Italy with one of my friends. We registered and prepared to attend a furniture exhibition which is held in Milan every year. We had a lot of exciting experiences during this trip. I enjoyed meeting new friends, discovering new places, and learning more about myself.

And during the trip, I had a little argument with my friend. I treat her like my big sister. We shared a happy companionship during this trip and got to know each other better. Although we argued at times while we were there, our friendship still remains because we learned to forgive and forget. We accept each other's opinions and enjoy our companionship.

The most important thing we learned is to be ourselves. That's how we maintained the friendship. Before the trip, we were planning to go to Venice, that famous place with the canals and gondolas. It's a romantic and unique place with a historical building that is surrounded by the sea. I was very blessed that my friend had a friend that offered us accommodation in Venice. We just needed to pay a few dollars for an agent fee. I discovered a lot of art that really opened my eyes and inspired me, especially in mosaics, glass, and painting.

Famous European art collector Peggy Guggenheim said, "I took advise from none but the best. I listened to how I listened! That's how I finally became my own expert." I was thinking of this collector who created her own business, doing things differently from others. That's why she is famous for her work. Travel is great to open our eyes to different cultures in other countries; it will also change your perspective. When traveling, be daring and ask directions. You will make friends with strangers, especially when you go alone.

My Adventure of Finding My Career Path

In my career as an interior designer, I've experienced a lot of challenges, especially right after my graduation as I went to my first job in Singapore. I encountered a lot of hardship in this industry along the way.

After graduation, I had a chance to go to Brunei with one of my friends who worked as a waitress. Three of us went to work at the new restaurant through my friend's connection.

We reached Brunei and settled into the accommodation that the company had provided. After a week, when the office supplied us the working pass, I learned that I could not be approved for the pass due to an age requirement. What a disappointing feeling! After a week of working, having fun, and making new friends, then I got the news that I needed to leave the country and my friend would stay. But this is the uncertainty of circumstances that we cannot predict.

A year later, I had another chance to work overseas in Singapore. With a lot of courage, I left Malaysia again. My parents were very supportive of me pursuing my dream and my career. They also did not worry too much because Singapore is a safe country—or we can say a peaceful country—that does not report a prevalence of common crimes. I also have relatives living there. I'm very fortunate that I still have a relative and friend here, unlike some of my friends who work here and have no one to really depend on. They are brave to leave their hometowns to pursue what they want and earn a living.

Singapore is a good place to advance one's career and has more job opportunities than many places. However, to come to Singapore for study and work was not an easy decision and path. I had only a little savings and my grandma gave me some pocket money. At that moment, I felt her love, which made it harder to leave home. I told her that I will be back home to visit her as time allows. I bought the ticket and flew to Singapore with my friend.

I stayed at my uncle's house temporarily until I got a job, and then I moved in with a friend sharing a room. I appreciate my friend who gave me a little guidance in finding a job. I decided to seek a position in the evening so that I could work at night while studying. After a few weeks of looking for a job, one of the molding companies offered to hire me in administration. Without overthinking, I accepted that job.

After one year of working while studying, I barely met my daily expenses because my salary was too low. I was crying and feeling sad because I couldn't earn enough money to save and take home. You would think that, working in Singapore, you would make good money, and the currency exchange is high. But due to expenses and the high cost of living, the money that I earned was not enough, and I was a foreigner in this country, a fresh graduate with no experience working in an office. The second year of working, I decided to change to a higher-paying position so that I could study. Finally, with courage, I enrolled in an interior design course to study part-time.

After two years of part-time study and work, I finally made a move into the interior design industry. I started to work as a sales designer as I was finishing my course that year. I decided to work in sales to learn more things which they didn't teach you in school, a lot of technical experience in this field. I really learned a lot. Then I hit rock bottom because of my unstable sales results, and, being on commission, I had no basic salary to meet my daily expenses and rental fees in Singapore. At that time I had a boyfriend and he was very supportive, helping me to pay for a few months of rent. After that, I decided to quit and pursue a job that paid a monthly salary.

A few years down the road, after changing jobs a few times, going from company to company earning valuable experience along the way, I was still searching for what I really wanted to do and what I hoped to achieve in the interior design industry. After searching, from out of nowhere, I came across a job in hospitality. An ex-boss and manager taught and guided me in this industry and really gave me a chance to explore and gain experience. Along with my journey in hospitality, I was glad that I was able to get to know a lot of good people who motivated me, and I got to know one of my managers who helped and taught me when I was making a mistake. I also received emotional support from a colleague to keep me going. Good colleagues are vital to provide understanding and help each other to complete each task.

After too many days and nights of working long hours, one day I felt I wanted to change my career and work in sales. Feeling lost, I was thinking I would further my studies overseas. At that moment, I was too tired and lost. Without thinking twice, I quit my job and went back to the freedom of target sales, and I was really lost.

With my income not stable and a lot of debt, too, I was feeling depressed and down. One of my friends took me to church, and instantly I felt peaceful, and I knew God would give me direction if I trusted him. So I started to look for a full-time job all over again. I found a company and a boss who appreciated my work, and we shared an appreciation for personal development and each other. I find that we need a purpose and a dream to help to keep us motivated while working.

During my time in direct sales, I had attended a lot of personal development courses. I learned a lot while working in direct sales. I learned how to deal and how to develop good communication skills. I developed the courage to approach strangers. I also had worked part-time at Starbucks where I learned their systematic processes.

Some people have too much ego and will not try different things because they are already committed to a profession. But for me to understand and learn different industries and the procedures and systems of work, especially in big companies, was helpful in my personal growth. I treated the various jobs as learning stages in the service industry and gained knowledge that money cannot buy. In *Rich Dad Poor Dad*, Robert Kiyosaki said that having people skills is important in any business. And he advised, **"When you are young, work to learn, not to earn."**

It is important that you love what you do. I still love what I am currently doing as an interior designer, grateful that I have completed a lot of interior designs of hotels and restaurants in India, China, Malaysia, and Singapore. Sometimes in life, we don't always think of ourselves and we focus on helping and inspiring others. I am even learning from my intent while working with others. Learn the way the young think and understand how they work, and courage them to pursue their dreams and desired careers.

> **To live by choice, not by chance.**
> **To be motivated, not manipulated.**
> **To be useful, not used.**
> **To make changes, not excuses.**
> **To excel, not compete.**
> **Choose self-esteem, not self-pity.**
>
> ~ Miranda Marrott

To listen to my inner voice, not to the random opinions of others. Choose to do the things that you won't so I am able to do the things you can't.

Showing up and Encouraging in Relationships

Everything in life is all about relationships with people, even at work, with co-workers, in business, and with family and friends.

Do you connect with a new person when you meet? There is a purpose in meeting a new friend or anyone who passes through your life. I think there is a purpose. I've overcome all the challenging situations and I continue to choose love and faith and to live in the present moment.

I met a guy who became my husband, and I knew him only for a short time before I realized that I was pregnant. We decided to have the child. I believe God gave this child to me as a gift. I felt ashamed for getting pregnant without being married first. Although in this century I know this is quite common, I preferred to have a good plan before having a child. I needed a lot of courage to adapt to the many changes that followed. I felt it was a blessing that I could have a child, as many married couples have tried to have children but are unable to.

During my pregnancy, I was changing jobs and, due to having a demanding boss, I was out of a job. I felt lost and worried—worried about expenses, bills, and the rent. I even had to pawn my gold. I contacted one of my ex-colleagues, and she helped me to get into her company on a contract basis. Thank God! I was safe and had a job until the delivery of my child. And I could cover my expenses and debt during that time.

This was not an easy period in my life. I am glad that I had an easy pregnancy and was surrounded by a lot of good friends that were encouraging and gave me a lot of support, both mentality and financially. I delivered my baby earlier than the due date. It was a blessing that I had my own room even though I didn't book from the hospital and delivered smoothly within two hours. I believe in the courage to have a natural childbirth.

It's true that I've had financial challenges due to the uncertainty of an unplanned marriage and childbirth. Sometimes I question myself: am I not good enough to be a mother or wife? But I am learning to be a mother to my child and a wife for my husband, too. No one is perfect and we learn from our mistakes. I choose to understand, listen, and love. Prayer keeps me in peace. And for now, I live happily, loved and enjoying life with my family. It takes courage to live an everyday life, we all deserve happiness simply because we are a human being. Onwards and upwards in courage.

"Courage is not simply
one of the virtues, but
the form of every virtue
at the testing point."

~ C.S Lewis

Author Biographies

John Spender

Chapter One

John Spender didn't learn how to read and write at a basic level until he was 10 years old. He has since traveled the world started many businesses leading him to create the best selling book series *A Journey Of Riches*, he is an Award Winning International Speaker and Movie Maker.

John was an international NLP trainer and has coached thousands of people from various backgrounds through all sorts of challenges. From the borderline homeless to very wealthy individuals, he has helped many people to get in touch with their truth to create a life on their terms.

John's search for answers to living a fulfilling life has taken him to working with Native American Indians in the Hills of San Diego, the forests of Madagascar, swimming with humpback whales in Tonga, exploring the Okavango Delta of Botswana and the Great Wall of China. He's traveled from Chile to Slovakia, Hungary to the Solomon Islands, the mountains of Italy and the streets of Mexico.

Everywhere his journey has taken him, John has discovered a hunger among people to find a new way to live, with a yearning for freedom.

He also co-wrote the script for the film 'Adversity and interviewed all the guests.

Frances Loughrey

CHAPTER TWO

Frances Loughrey is currently based primarily in Melbourne, Australia but has recently led a nomadic existence, including living for a spell in Bali and Thailand.

From the UK, she plans to spend much more time there in future and looks forward to living in various locations over the coming years. With a portfolio career which includes personal coaching and organisational training, writing and speaking, Frances is determined that neither age nor distance will stop her from making choices that allow her to experience life in a deliberate way rather than just going through the motions. Her friends invariably describe her as determined, resilient, adventurous and fun while she likes to think of herself as intelligent, sophisticated and adaptable!

The I.D.E.A.L.L. Program is one of the ways she shares her experience and knowledge with others through workshops and retreats and this year has launched her first ever foray into the world of online courses.

www.floughreycoaching.com.au

floughreycoaching@gmail.com

Francisca X Ruiz

CHAPTER THREE

Francisca is the mother of two beautiful young women that have become her greatest teachers. She received her business degree in International Business Administration at Bergen and her RE broker's license at Kovats RE school in New Jersey.

She then built a career, creating solutions in Commercial Real Estate where she identified lucrative projects for investors in the NJ, NY and Florida markets.

Her degree was in Business, but her passion was music. Playing classical piano as well as teaching and transposing for latin bands, was a driving force to stay connected to her soul.

Francisca found that her journey on this planet was deeper than the day to day grind in Real Estate. In following her adventurous souls desires she was guided to Network

Marketing. Through this avenue, she has been able to realize how free and creative her life could be. She realized how fulfilling it was for her to help others achieve that same freedom in guiding them to seek their greatest soul purpose. Francisca soon shifted her focus to providing sessions with her spiritual guides. She incorporated angel readings and modalities generationally gifted to hold space for others. Francisca is a student of life with a passion for sharing how magical and divine humanity is in today's world.

Her connection to source and humanity is a conscious reminder of how we are all beautiful in our messy ways. She believes we all come together and cross paths in this domain called planet Earth with a unique purpose, to experience and fulfill our soul's karma. For all of the lessons learned thus far she is infinitely grateful, accepting the hard times and pain with as much grace as the good. She continues evolving into a greater space of love and light and a life of service.

Laura Hyman

CHAPTER FOUR

Laura grew up in Venice California and now resides in Etowah N.C. with her husband of 39 years, Myron.

They have three beautiful married daughters and five grandchildren. They both are retired and decided to start living a healthy lifestyle and put themselves first. They both are members of the 100 Pound Club, Laura is a Founding Growth Leader with Growth-U, and enjoys helping others create healthy minds and bodies, by using the cycle of growth and the laws of focus and Nutritional Cleansing.

Laura was a Manicurist for over 30 years and a caregiver for her Mother-in-law for four years and then for her own mother until they both passed away. Laura and Myron are living life out loud and to the fullest and showing everyone that it's never too late to start caring for yourself. Sharing the tools to create the life you choose. #oursonghasjustbegun and so has yours!!

Dr. Neelu Parihar

Chapter Five

Dr. Neelu Parihar is a vibrant and courageous personality with a flair for sailing through life's trying times. Even after a challenging background, she completed her doctorate in the field of physiotherapy, and after a brief stint of working in a job, she went on to establish a healthcare business of her own.

She eventually converted the business into a thriving franchise and has also recently ventured into the corporate world with a role that allows her to travel extensively. As a self-taught entrepreneur and a master of personal finance, her learning curve has been shaped by her life experiences and values. Dr. Neelu is also an avid traveling enthusiast.

She aims to cover every unchartered territory in the world with her partner.

Susan Campbell Nickels

CHAPTER SIX

Susan Lynn Campbell-Nickels was raised in Hacienda Heights, California. She now resides in Oakhurst, California near the gateway to Yosemite National Park. Her two beautiful children, Janet and John, are now living their own life stories.

Susan is married to Rich, the man of her dreams and step-father to her two children. Presently an Account Executive with Sierra Seafood, a wholesale seafood and shellfish distributor, in Oakhurst, California. She has been employed for over fifteen years working with an incredible team providing the finest seafood throughout the Central Valley and mountain communities.

Susan has a home-based nutrition business with a passion for freeing people from physical and financial pain because she believes our health is our greatest wealth. In 1979 Susan received her Associate of Arts degree from Mount San Antonio College in Walnut, California. With her focus on photography, she was honored to be Student Assistant for a photography class at the Chaminade University of Honolulu, Hawaii.

Susan enjoys the great outdoors, appreciates all the beauty that surrounds her and lives life to the fullest. Faith, Hope and Love is her favorite motto. Susan hobbies include socializing, bird watching, reading, manifesting, meditating/ praying, earthing and her favorite, photography. Smile!

Contact information
Susan Campbell Nickels
P.O. Box 691
Oakhurst, California
93644
Email
suezq@sti.net

Haimchand Katwaroo

CHAPTER SEVEN

Haimchand was born in Guyana, raised in Winnipeg, Canada, and currently resides in Toronto, Canada. He has a Bachelor of Science Degree (Majoring in Mathematics and Physics) and a Bachelor of Commerce Degrees (Majoring in Finance and Marketing). He has had success as a professional financial advisor with one of Canada's major banks, and in sales roles with a variety of industries.

In 2003, Haimchand purchased Toronto Furnished Apartments and increased the sales of the company by 500% over the next 14 years. Before the sale of the company, Toronto Furnished Apartments was one of the five biggest corporate housing providers in the Greater Toronto Area.

Haimchand has always set high expectations for himself. One of his most private goals is to retire as early as possible and start a charitable foundation that will help underprivileged children. He currently participates in a variety of charity organizations donating both time and money. His driving points in life are to achieve financial success for himself and his family and to use that financial success to help those who are less fortunate. He believes that one must first learn and understand themselves before you can help others.

After the sale of the company, Haimchand has focused on a portfolio of private investments and taking the time to travel around the world. His next goal will be to register The Katwaroo Foundation as a registered charity in Canada.

Theresa Rodriguez

CHAPTER EIGHT

Theresa Rodriguez currently lives in South Carolina with her husband, Richard, and their three amazing children, but you won't always find them here, as they love the freedom of the open road and spend much of their time traveling.

Though she has her hands full as a homeschooling mom who runs her own business, she still finds the time and energy to make it a priority to bring light to those around her by inspiring, motivating, and guiding people towards healthy living and being true to themselves.

Being someone who practices minimum living, she loves the simplicity of life, enjoying time in nature with her family, drinking coffee with friends, and attempting to unravel the mysteries of the universe.

Donna Pearl

Chapter Nine

Donna Cotterell is an educator, writer, producer, director, actress and activist who resides in Tallahassee, Florida. She has a B.A. in Theatre Arts from the University of Massachusetts in Boston, a M.S. in Administrative Studies from Boston University and a M.Ed. With a concentration in Middle School Mathematics from Lesley University in Cambridge, Massachusetts.

Founder and Director of both Indaba Theatre of New England and Indaba Theatre of Florida; which are 501(c)3 nonprofit organizations, she was selected as one of Brockton, Massachusetts Women of the Year in 2012. She is currently working on a theater project in Tallahassee, Florida titled "Marigold Day's - Conversations of Change" a series of performances created to foster dialogue around social justice issues. Her inspirational speaking has brought her to South Africa, India and Indonesia.

Alice Ho

CHAPTER TEN

Alice Ho A.H from Borneo East Malaysia, Sarawak. She carried a harmonize and tolerance personality where she was born.

Currently living in Singapore for more than 10 years working as an Interior Designer FF&E specialist in project management. She is passionate about creative art, painting, cartoonist drawing and handicraft.

Alice has a good eye for color and contributes to the place and people who she works with. A health conscious and lover of the environment friendly campaign, She likes to share and to connect with other people.

Alice carries a positive mindset, adventurous, curious, and a looking forward attitude. Like as Alice In Wonderland. "Begin at the beginning, and ended fruitfully." Determination and daring make her successful in going through life and pursue her dreams.

www.tmisaliceho.com misalicedesigner@gmail.com

"Don't dream your life,
but live your dream."

~ Mark Twain

AFTERWORD

I hope you enjoyed the collection of heartfelt stories, wisdom and vulnerability shared. Storytelling is the oldest form of communication, and I hope you feel inspired to take a step toward living a fulfilling life. Feel free to contact any of the authors in this book or the other books in this series.

The proceeds of this book will go to the Bali Street Kids Project, in Denpasar, Bali.

The project gives orphaned and abandoned children a home, meals and an education.

You can donate to this fantastic cause here: http://ykpa.org/

Other books in the series are...

The Power Healing : A Journey of Riches, Book Fifteen

https://www.amazon.com/dp/B07LGRJQ2S

The Way of the Entrepreneur: A Journey Of Riches, Book Fourteen

https://www.amazon.com/dp/B07KNHYR8V

Discovering Love and Gratitude: A Journey Of Riches, Book Thirteen

https://www.amazon.com/dp/B07H23Q6D1

Transformational Change: A Journey Of Riches, Book Twelve

https://www.amazon.com/dp/B07FYHMQRS

Finding Inspiration: A Journey Of Riches, Book Eleven

https://www.amazon.com/dp/B07F1LS1ZW

Building your Life from Rock Bottom: A Journey Of Riches, Book Ten

https://www.amazon.com/dp/B07CZK155Z

Transformation Calling: A Journey Of Riches, Book Nine

https://www.amazon.com/dp/B07BWQY9FB

Letting Go and Embracing the New: A Journey Of Riches, Book Eight

https://www.amazon.com/dp/B079ZKT2C2

Making Empowering Choices: A Journey Of Riches, Book Seven

https://www.amazon.com/Making-Empowering-Choices-Journey-Riches-ebook/dp/B078JXMK5V

The Benefit of Challenge: A Journey Of Riches, Book Six

https://www.amazon.com/dp/B0778S2VBD

Personal Changes: A Journey Of Riches, Book Five

https://www.amazon.com/dp/B075WCQM4N

Dealing with Changes in Life: A Journey Of Riches, Book Four

https://www.amazon.com/dp/B0716RDKK7

Making Changes: A Journey Of Riches, Book Three

https://www.amazon.com/dp/B01MYWNI5A

The Gift In Challenge: A Journey Of Riches, Book Two

https://www.amazon.com/dp/B01GBEML4G

From Darkness into the Light: A Journey Of Riches, Book One

https://www.amazon.com/dp/B018QMPHJW

Thank you to all the authors that have shared aspects of their lives in the hope that it will inspire others to live a bigger version of themselves. I heard a great saying from Jim Rohan "You can't complain and feel grateful at the same time" at any given moment we have a chose to either feel like a victim of life or connected and grateful for it. I hope this book helps you to feel grateful and go after your dreams.